Cross my Heart

Cross my Heart
Ferne McCann

arrow books

1 3 5 7 9 10 8 6 4 2

Arrow Books
20 Vauxhall Bridge Road
London SW1V 2SA

Arrow Books is part of the Penguin Random House group of companies
whose addresses can be found at global.penguinrandomhouse.com.

First published in Great Britain in 2016 by Century

Published by Arrow Books 2016

www.penguin.co.uk

A CIP catalogue record for this book is available
from the British Library.

ISBN 9781784755744

Typeset in 11.6/17.82 pt Minion
Jouve (UK), Milton Keynes
Printed and bound in Great Britain by Clays Ltd, St Ives plc

Penguin Random House is committed to a sustainable future for our
business, our readers and our planet. This book is made from Forest
Stewardship Council® certified paper.

To our beautiful Ronnie who has given us all a wonderful new chapter. I can't wait for your story.

Contents

Prologue

'What the hell? The whole thing? How?!'

I hid my face behind my hands as Ant and Dec announced (with a lot of laughing and a real sense of glee in their voices): 'Yes, the whole thing. It's a live water spider.'

As the lid came off the serving dish I couldn't believe the size of it. This was no house spider slipping down the plughole of the bath at home in Essex – it was *huge*. It was also pretty angry at being trapped in a glass, and its legs were going everywhere, it wouldn't stop moving. I had no idea how I would swallow this monster and I wanted to be properly sick. I'd expected disgusting stuff for the final as they always save the worst until last, but I didn't expect the 'food' to be alive.

When I watch the clip back I laugh now at the faces I make: I do a sort of grin when I am nervous or anxious, like I can't quite believe what's happening. I certainly couldn't believe this was how I would be ending my time in the jungle. Ant and Dec told me to swirl it round in the bottom of the glass so that its legs would curl up. This would mean the spider would shrink into a smaller ball that would be easier to swallow.

It didn't. I sat there shaking the glass round in big circles and screamed every time it touched the palm of my hand. It just didn't get any smaller and its legs made an awful sound as they hit the side of the glass. I had one last scream as I knocked it back, telling myself it was just like the shots I would down on a night out. There are no words to describe how gross it was. I was smashing my clenched fists against the table to distract myself from the taste as I crunched my way through the horror. No matter how hard I chewed, it wouldn't go down. Ant and Dec were loving it and I just couldn't believe it was alive in my mouth. Of all the trials I had endured, this was the ultimate horror.

There was a huge amount of pressure in being given the job of bringing home the main course – the clue is in the word 'main' – it was the key element to the last meal we were going to win in the jungle.

But I knew I just had to crack on. I had survived three weeks in the jungle and done six trials – I was determined I wouldn't fall at the final hurdle and utter those words: 'I'm a celebrity . . . Get me out of here!' The one thing I'd promised myself before I went in was that, whatever happened and no matter how bad it got, those words would never come out of my mouth. To be honest, I don't think the viewers expected many of the words that did actually come out of my mouth. I'm not stupid – I know that before I went in people had their opinions of me and that lots of them weren't nice. I understood that and could see why. Being on a show like *The Only Way is Essex* is always going to leave you open to criticism. People think if you are in a reality show they know everything about you, but that couldn't be further from the truth. *TOWIE* is great entertainment, but it's only that.

Going into the jungle was extreme, but it needed to be in order for people to see the actual person behind the headlines and the social media profile. It was my first chance, since I'd crashed on to TV screens in 2013 at the age of twenty-two, to show the real me, the Ferne my friends and family knew was always going to be 100 per cent at home in the wilderness: hair scraped back in a scrunchie, not washing, mucking in with the chores and

3

taking an interest in everyone around me. There wasn't a moment in that camp that I didn't feel grateful for and that I didn't love; I'd do it all over again right now if I could. It was the most special time, a chance to step away from the creation that I'd become, a chance to be away from myself, really. Those weeks in the jungle were truly some of the happiest of my life and I spent every minute I was there pinching myself to believe it was real. I know it sounds like a cliché when people who enter a competition say there is no way they will win (to be honest, you just think they are covering themselves in case they are out first!), but trust me, in my case it's totally true: there is no way I'd ever imagined making it past the first week, never mind to the final.

It was a show I'd dreamed about getting on. I genuinely felt that if only one person out there got to see my real character and changed their mind about me it would have been worth it. I think part of the reason I did it was to show people that I wasn't just about tears and being in the middle of the drama – there really is so much more to me than Essex aggravation. I am a total team player and there was no better environment to show that. I love the outdoors, I love people, I love working hard, cooking and talking – what could go wrong?

I guess that's sort of how I feel about this book. It's a big thing to do when you're young and knowing you have to talk about memories you thought you'd lost or things that are private. It just feels like the right time to show a side that so many viewers haven't seen, to set the record straight, to take you to the mad planet of Ferne McCann. Don't get me wrong – I am nervous, but I'm going to live by my motto: 'Feel the fear and do it anyway.'

1

Once Upon a Time . . .

It always winds me up when people say Essex folk are thick and lazy, that we just bum around getting sunbeds, gluing on false nails and prancing up and down Brentwood High Street waiting to be noticed. Don't get me wrong, some do think they are celebrities (especially the Essex boys), but before *TOWIE* I wasn't a kid on the lookout for fame or living in a dodgy area I was desperate to escape. In fact, my childhood was picture perfect until my parents divorced when I was thirteen.

I'm an Essex girl through and through and proud to be so, but I don't think my early childhood is necessarily typical of what people might think. My dad was a very successful trader in the City – it was all quite *Wolf of Wall*

Street – and we really lived the life. I was born in Harold Wood and I lived in Brentwood. We had a beautiful big house with five bedrooms and I suppose, if I am honest, I didn't really recognise how lucky I was until it was taken away. That was the house I came home to after I was born and that was my home until my parents split up and we had to move out, taking only our memories with us.

I suppose I did recognise that things were slightly different for us. I do remember being about seven years old and being dropped back home after a play date. I was in the back of the car with two friends and their eyes were out on stalks as we drew up outside the house. I guess that old saying about not knowing what you've got until it's gone is true after all, but I know we were very lucky.

In many ways we were a typical 2.4 family – no real drama. (I brought plenty of that to the table much later!) I grew up with my sister Sophie, who, despite being three years older than me, was my best friend (still is). We always used to joke that technically I shouldn't be here, as my mum had an ectopic pregnancy after my sister was born and before I was conceived. Mum had always been adamant there would only ever be two children, so I was a near miss. Imagine that, life without Ferne – it doesn't bear thinking about! We were close as children, embarrassingly my mum used to dress us the same, which stopped being so cute the older we got. We did lots together, though, and Mum gave us freedom, she let us be ourselves, and I think of my childhood as being very joyful – our house was a happy house and I grew up in a lively household with lots of people about and lots of love.

My dad is very charismatic and everyone wants to be his friend. He has always been the life and soul of the party and I see so much of him in me when it comes to being sociable and creating the party feeling. My friends often say that my mad party vibe is missed if I'm not around for a night out. I throw myself into having a good time and making sure everyone else does too – I definitely get that from him.

Dad loved having people round and the overriding memory of my childhood are the amazing parties my parents threw on Friday and Saturday nights at the house. They were great hosts and I know that has massively rubbed off on me and my sister – when I get my own place I know it will be brimming with people all the time. They were both great cooks and I recall the smell of food cooking and hearing wine corks popping as Simply Red or Sade played in the background. Sometimes there were daytime barbecues with all the kids, but mostly the socialising went on in the evenings when we were supposed to be in bed. But I would peer in, dreaming about what grown-up life would be like for me one day.

My parents' marriage was definitely picture perfect from the outside. But I suppose, like any relationship, it depends from which angle you are looking – study it too hard and you will definitely see the flaws. I think if my mum is honest she would say that she was unhappy for some of my early years, that she felt suppressed and that life could be a lot about what my dad wanted.* By nature Mum is a very bubbly and cheeky person when you get to know her but, at the beginning, she can wrongly come across as a bit reserved. I think that's because for years she was never really allowed to look as if she was the one having fun. I'm not sure of the psychology behind it all, but I think perhaps my dad liked the attention on him. In many ways maybe he was just being a typical Essex

---

* I obviously don't know the ins and outs but I'm sure there were times my dad felt unhappy too. There are two people in every marriage after all.

bloke – he doesn't mean anything by it and he's a kind and fun guy who likes nothing more than seeing people have a good time. But Essex ways can rub off on people, especially the boys; as you have probably seen over the years on the show, it's all about them and they expect their women to respect that.

I can't really remember when the arguments actually started but they were hard to ignore – kids notice absolutely everything; parents always think they are good at covering stuff up but, believe me, nothing escapes us! You know that scenario when your mum and dad are arguing and they have both really got the hump. Then one of them grabs the car keys and shouts: 'I need some air' (or something equally clichéd). Well, I was that kid on the bottom of the stairs getting involved in the drama, screaming as though someone was going to die and the world was going to end: 'Don't leave, please don't leave!' Whoever left always came back and I could never sleep until I heard the front door close and the click of the key as the lock was turned.

My dad had taken to staying up in London and going out for drinks after work. He lived the typical trader life – he left before 7am to get the train before I woke up and would be back after I'd gone to bed. I took his absence out on my mum, as she was the one always around and in charge of discipline. I was such a daddy's girl until my parents divorced – he was my hero and could do no wrong. It's funny how things change as you get older. Don't get me wrong, I love my dad so much, but now I would literally die for my mum and I have so much respect for the way she's managed her own life and how strong she has been. She's put up with so much (including terrible teen behaviour from me, but more on that later). She is amazing.

But my parents couldn't hide their troubles – the cracks started to show and I noticed that my mum was sleeping in another room. I remember asking her why she was sleeping in the spare bedroom. Her reply was always the same: 'Dad's snoring is keeping me awake.'

Mum has hinted that she was never convinced her marriage was all it could have been – I'm not sure that as she walked up the aisle she was as thrilled about becoming a wife as she should have been. My parents met at a bus stop when they were seventeen, and my mum was bowled over by my dad. They dated for eight years before eventually getting married, I think it just seemed the next logical step. That's not to say there weren't loads of happy times – there were, and I grew up in a loving home – but perhaps the break-up happening at such a tricky age had a more lasting effect on me than I realised. They had their issues, but that's their story to tell and they will obviously both have different opinions. For me, I think it has really affected how I behave around blokes. I suppose you could argue that their divorce formed some of the patterns of behaviour that relationships bring out in me (much more on that later). It wasn't that the environment was damaging, I think perhaps it was more the fact that I felt abandoned and a huge sense of loss when my father left and it made me insecure about my worth when it came to blokes.

It didn't take long to expose the whole 'snoring and separate room' sham – Sophie and I soon realised they were living separately. To be more accurate, we discovered they weren't together any more when we found out that dad was seeing someone else.

Now, to be clear and fair to my dad, he had done *nothing* wrong as he and Mum weren't together any more. But when you're aged thirteen and sixteen, I'm not sure that logic or fairness is necessarily applied. Well, it wasn't in our case – Sophie and I thought it needed exposing, and we were just the girls for the job. So we did the most unhelpful and teenage thing we could think of: we decided we were going to call the woman.

We were like two really bad private detectives, creeping into Dad's study and going through his contacts. We knew she was called Sara, and there she was in his Filofax, so we dialled. As the oldest, Sophie was in charge; I couldn't be trusted, to be honest, as I was far less calm about the whole thing. Those three years between us made all the difference and she understood far more that it wasn't an affair if Mum and Dad were separated. It didn't stop her naughty side coming out, though. Sophie dialled the number and put the phone on speaker. She was ringing this woman! I couldn't believe it.

Sophie put on her best phone voice and said: 'Hello, is that Sara? It's Sophie and Ferne here, Simon's daughters. Is my dad there, please?' There was a pause and a lot of crackling before Dad picked up the phone and sheepishly said hello. That was all the confirmation we needed that our parents' marriage was over.

It turned out that my dad and Sara were perfect for each other really – they were both into the same things like gardening, the outdoors and dogs, they were so compatible and really in love. She was definitely the person he should have been with, his 'one'. It was so sad what happened in the end: they did get together and get married and were really happy, but Sara was diagnosed with cancer and died at a very young age. It was such a sad time as they were really good together for five years, even though Sara was ill for quite a lot of that. Their big plan was to retire and buy an amazing dairy farm, Deer Park, and do it up. Dad is still living that dream for her now.

But before all that, things were changing at home and before I knew it, my parents had decided that sharing the house wasn't working. Looking back, I don't think I processed it properly – I just got really angry and I took it out on my mum. I worshipped my dad and I suppose I unfairly blamed her for them breaking up as, in the end, it was Mum who initiated the split. I'm sure loads of kids who've been through their parents breaking up will identify with that. You are just desperate for things to stay the same. You want your parents together for ever and you don't understand that people fall out of love and grow apart, and that you aren't enough to keep them together. In my parents' case, there was no great drama, no bitter collapse. Over the course of four to five years they just realised they weren't meant to be together, but you never understand that as a child. I suppose it was the moment I realised I wasn't one of those people who could mask my feelings easily: us all moving out of our house hurt and I made sure everyone knew it.

2

Spicy Clothes and Scruffy Ways

My mum always used to say that I was her beautiful little tink – with an older sister and her friends, I was certainly used to be being pushed and pulled all over the place and bossed around. So starting St Peter's Primary School and being adopted in the playground by the older girls meant I was in my element; I was like a living toy for them and I loved it.

I was quite a tomboy; I suppose I still am really. I remember being aged about eight and wearing a disgusting Adidas navy-blue jumper with a high round neck. I wore it everywhere, all the time, and my mum cut my hair in this little bob. I looked like a dainty boy – there were certainly no hair extensions back then! Looking back, it's fair to say that I had a real issue with clothes and hated getting my hair cut; once I threw myself down on the salon floor in a tantrum and nearly knocked myself out. I hated wearing clothes. It's not as if I wanted to go around naked all the time, more that I hated putting freshly washed clothes on. In fact, clean clothes made me really angry! I made so much fuss and wore that rank jumper all the time.

Once my mum came into my room and sat on the end of my bed with a pile of freshly ironed clothes. I refused to have them near me and I remember her saying: 'Why, why, why?'

My answer was comedy: 'I don't know, they just feel spicy and itchy on my skin and they hurt.' What a nutter, who describes clean clothes as spicy.

Even now, although I like my nice clothes and handbags, I'm not a typical girly girl. Give me a pair of old jeans and a T-shirt and I'm happy. It was another reason I was in my element in the jungle: there's nothing I love more than a pyjama day or scraping my hair back and wearing my gym kit. Getting all glammed up is part of the job (no one wants me Instagramming my non-made-up face), but the real me is happier with bare skin and a ponytail. Much as I love my lashes and nails, somehow

I still always manage to look scruffy even when I am glammed up! I have always been that way, even as a child. My mum would get me ready for school, giving me the perfect French plait, and by the time I walked from the car to the school gate it would be out, hair hanging down in my face. I didn't ever want to look perfect, I wanted to be different.

Believe it or not, I was a really shy child. (I know!) Mum tells me that I really didn't like nursery school much when I started and insisted that the teachers cuddle me on their laps and generally make a fuss of me, but primary school was a whole different ball game. There is a long-running family joke that I started St Peter's in Brentwood, just down the road from our house, as a quiet, smiley girl who people often patted on the head and looked past, but by the time I left that place, there wasn't a pupil, teacher or parent who didn't know who I was. At one end of term play I had a solo and so did another boy in my class. As we took our bows, I saw one mum point her finger at us and say: 'Those two up there, mark my words, they will be famous.' I don't know what the boy is doing now, but I always remember her saying that and wondering if the choices we make are partly fate.

Sophie and I were best friends with Robyn and Daniel.

(Sophie was a bridesmaid for Robyn when she got married.) Our parents met when we all started at primary school and we would go on holiday with them all the time. It was lovely, the four of us going away together, going up on the stage at the holiday clubs and playing in the pool and on the beach – we are still all really close and I love them both.

I really don't know when I stopped being that shy girl and became more confident in myself, but I do remember the realisation that I could entertain people. It was never arrogance, but more the wish to make the people around me laugh and be happy. Later on you could see that side of me very much on show in the jungle: I would often distract some of the bigger personalities with humour and banter to diffuse a situation. I know given how I came across on *TOWIE* you might laugh at this, but I genuinely have always hated confrontation and do anything to avoid it.

I won't lie – I've never been the world's sharpest academic tool, but I always did fine. I think my problem has always been that I take that bit longer to process information and probably needed some things explaining to me more than once. But once I discovered my dramatic side there was no stopping me, and what I might have lacked in the classroom I certainly made up for on the stage with my imagination. Perhaps I needed an outlet; whatever it was, my creative streak never let me down – I was always doing something. I'm sure my mum must have despaired at times. There was always a show in the living room or the garden; even when I wasn't performing I sang or danced or talked non-stop, like that toy in the box you want to take the battery out of.

I also showed early signs of throwing everything I had at boys when I liked them. There was a boy called Richard who I really liked in year 6. I used to hang on his every word and be desperate for him to like me back. I remember deciding the best way to get his attention was to give him all the money I had from my piggy bank! So I made a card for him and sellotaped all these pound coins and coppers into it. It was everything I had and I wanted him to have it.* He didn't seem that impressed when I gave it to him and the next day his mum gave it back to my mum as it had all my pocket money in it. A few days later we were playing together in his house and he was whacking me over the head with his tie, so I am

---

* Even at a young age I would literally give everything – I am all or nothing.

not sure my great romantic gesture made the impression I was hoping for!

My sister actually did more drama at school than me, but I got into it too and I liked nothing more than losing myself in an imaginary world of plays and make-believe. When I put on shows at home I demanded the full attention of my audience. Nothing less would do and there was no way Mum was allowed to multitask with something like the ironing – *all* eyes had to be on me!

Despite how things appeared in *TOWIE*, I have always been lucky with my friends – I never really struggled to make any and I've always been a girls' girl. I was popular at primary school and never had any trouble finding and keeping friends. I think if my friends were asked to sum me up in one word they would say 'loyal' – there's nothing I wouldn't do for my close friends and I always have their backs. I can't stand bullying or unfairness, a side I don't think *TOWIE* was very good at showing. I am fierce in my friendships and I don't ever give up on people without a good reason; my girls mean the world to me.

That ease with friendship saw me through my early school years and set me up well for secondary school, which is where I found my group of six who are still my best mates to this day. I absolutely adored all my school years – I don't know what it was, but I loved being part of a community and I threw myself into everything at secondary school. It was there that I discovered my real love for sport, netball in particular. My dad had been very sporty and great at hockey when he was young and I don't know if that's where I get it from, but I have always loved my sport and being part of a team. I've always believed in the power of numbers.

Making friends came naturally. People have genuinely always wanted me around, although in *TOWIE* there were times when no one liked me apart from Billie. That was a complicated side to the show that I will talk about later, but it's one of the biggest misconceptions people have about me. I am not a hater – in fact, that couldn't be further from the truth.

Since I was on the show, people have said a lot of things. One of the things they say most often is that I like to be liked. I suppose that's partly true, mainly because, until I went on the show, I had my friends and being judged really wasn't an issue. I had a natural group but I was never at the top of the pecking order, never the ringleader, but I always felt an important part of the gang.

I throw myself into everything I do and *TOWIE* was no different. I gave absolutely everything to that show and in the end I knew how to work it. I pushed the stories forward and asked the questions the audience wanted answers to, and I definitely paid the price. Part of that suffering was being portrayed as someone who couldn't make, or hang on to, friends. Anyone who knew me back in my schooldays would know that wasn't true.

I have always found it so easy to strike up conversation. You could be next to me on a plane or a train – anywhere I am and no matter who I'm with – and I'd always have something to say. That is mostly down to the fact that I started a job when I was fourteen years old in the local hairdresser's. It was definitely one of those sink-or-swim scenarios: being a Saturday girl in a salon, you couldn't afford to run out of chat. I like to think it's sort of fate that I ended up in the jungle, the place where I most needed that chatty quality. That camp was full of interesting types, and how often do you get stranded with so many people from different walks of life? I couldn't imagine getting through that whole experience and not asking everyone loads of questions. Some might find it nosy, but I am genuinely a very curious person who is interested in other people. I know it comes from listening to all those customers in the salon talking about what they'd been up to, what jobs they had, boyfriend trouble – you name it, we'd talk about it. I got the job a year after my parents had split - it was like a lifeline to help escape the sadness and it really helped me learn stuff about myself.

I also think that confidence in striking up chat came partly from having my girls and knowing they were always there for me, no matter what. My special six are like my family – we've seen each other through every drama, high and low and everything in between. I will always be grateful I had them by my side when, at the age of thirteen, my parents finally divorced. That support came especially from Billie Faiers.

Deep down I knew things couldn't go on as they were at home, but when it did all end one of the biggest things was having to move out of our house. When they officially divorced, because they'd been separated for so long, Dad was seeing Sara and she lived in Surrey at the time. It was decided that he would move there with her, Mum and Dad would sell the house and Mum would find somewhere else to live with me and my sister. I was thirteen and Sophie was sixteen when the family house was sold. I remember so clearly the last night we had in that house.

Billie called me on the landline – this was long before

the days of iPhones and being able to talk in private. I'm talking about the days where I used to be on the house phone for hours at a time so that no one else could use it. I would talk to my friends all night long (even though I'd spent all day with them) and we used to spend all evening talking through every detail of the day we'd just spent together. When the phone rang that night it was just like any other. My mum shouted: 'It's Billie, Ferne!'

I would take the phone to my bedroom so that I could settle in for a long gossip. I still know Billie's childhood landline number off by heart even today because I dialled it so often. That night, though, Billie knew I was gutted to be leaving the house and that I was finding it hard. I stood in my lovely bedroom, with the sunflowers on the wall that Dad had spray-painted on, with everything in boxes, and I felt lost. I'll never forget what Billie said to me: 'Listen, Ferne, I've been thinking. I know you are going through a really rough time at the moment and I can't even imagine how horrible it is for you. But I want you to know that I'm always here for you, no matter what, and you can come here any time if you hate the new house. You can come here at the weekends and just stay the whole time. I will always be here for you, I just want you to know that.'

I think back now and I'm amazed that Billie could think and act so maturely, at the age of thirteen. But she has always had my back and stuck up for me. Even when I've been my own worst enemy and made it hard for her, she has never cut me loose or been disloyal. I'm sure there are times she has wanted to, but she's stuck by me and I am so grateful for her loyalty – that night as her thirteen-year-old self was just one example.

Later, when we were on the show, people used to say to me: 'Why does Billie never stick up for you on camera?' To be fair, looking back on some scenarios I was filmed in, I think anyone would have found it hard to chime in on my behalf. But for me that's never been the point. Billie is a fierce friend and I have never needed her to prove it by getting herself involved in some of the show-generated aggravation. That's not what we're about and we both know that.

Anyway, her calling me that night before the move meant so much and I still think about it to this day. The next morning was moving day and I was sent to school as usual. I set off, leaving the only home I'd ever had, in the morning and in the afternoon I was picked up from school and taken to our new house.

I won't lie, I thought the new house was really shabby

when we first got there. Funnily enough, Mum recently confessed that when she bought it she thought: Oh God, what have I done?

We had left Brentwood for Shenfield and lived in that new house for just over a year. Although Dad still worked in Essex, because he lived in Surrey Sophie and I never really did that whole 'every other weekend with your dad' thing. We just stayed with Mum really. I suppose that had a big impact on my relationship with my dad. When you're that age, every day has a different drama and if you aren't there for it, the distance kicks in really quickly. Dad would sometimes call up after school to see if we fancied dinner out, but my sister and me were at the age when we were never in – having no plans was sad and so we were always busy. There was never time for a last-minute dinner date with Dad. That distance doubled when he eventually moved to Surrey. Life was different but not in a good way. I was living in a house I hated with my mum as a single parent.

I know that I started acting up around this time. Imagine the combination of me, hormones and the upset of what was happening at home – it was a nightmare! But my friends were there, 100 per cent. There are lots of memories that stand out around this time, and one is

Billie's kindness. We have always said that Billie is a wise girl – she's always been more mature than the rest of us for her age. She could see I was hurting and, typical Bill, she tried to make it better, but sometimes I didn't help myself.

There was one time my friends all thought I was getting out of hand and so they staged some kind of intervention on me. They came to find me at lunchtime, sat me down and had really serious faces on: they had real stuff to say. There was a nominated spokesperson, and I sat back as they listed my crimes: 'Listen, we know you've been going through a hard time lately, but you've been out of order. You burst Steph's birthday balloon the other day, which was not on, so you need to get her a new one. You also borrowed a couple of quid off Billie last week, so you need to pay that back.'

It went on and on: 'you did this, you said that', and as petty as it seems, I remember just feeling overwhelmed and really confused but knowing that I had to put it right. To be honest, I wasn't even sure I'd done these things as life was a bit of a blur at that point. But, I knew I wanted to set everything straight and had to sort it asap – these girls were my life and the last thing I wanted to do was hurt them. I went home and told my mum.

(Despite me being a right pain we were really close and I always told her all my worries.)

As mums do, she could immediately see the pain and upset the divorce was causing me. Like a magician she produced a balloon from a half-open packet she had. She gave it to me and went over to her wallet, where she produced a few pound coins and put them into an envelope, and she placed all of this into my school bag. That was my protective mum: she knew I'd been a pain lately, but she also knew I was having a hard time readjusting and she thought I should be cut some slack and she fixed the problem in an instant.

But that small blip was my friends' way of keeping me on the straight and narrow, and I trust those girls with my life. Little did I know Billie and I would have far more drama later in life, this time on the TV screen for everyone to see.

3

The Class Clown

In a way, school became the perfect escape from dealing with my new home life situation, although it didn't really translate into me doing well in the classroom. Despite the fact that it was a mixed comprehensive, we were split into single-sex classes for years 7, 8 and 9. It was a bit like having the best of both worlds, the boys in the playground but your girl mates around you all the time.

I can't remember when I discovered that acting the clown made people laugh, and I don't really know why I did it. I reckon if you were to ask any of my classmates what they remember most about me, it would be that I was always mucking around and trying to make people laugh. I suppose if I got deep, I might argue that it was to distract me from the upheaval at home, though I don't remember that being the reason in my head at the time. I genuinely just liked to make people laugh and didn't even mind getting the after-school detentions for it. My feeling was that, if everyone had a laugh, then it was worth getting punished. I was detention queen and it still makes me laugh that, after getting ten after-school detentions in a row, I was punished with another detention!

I don't think it was attention-seeking or a deliberate wish to be disruptive (though some might disagree, and I *was* disruptive). I think I'm just a bit of a practical joker and used humour as an escape; I always have and that hasn't changed as I've got older. Whatever the intention, it got me into trouble and I was labelled as a bad influence. Any understanding and cutting of slack because of the divorce only stretched so far, and one day Mum was called into the school by Miss Pridham, my head of year. She was not happy. I can't pretend I liked her much – to me she was just a moaner who wore cardigans and told us off all the time. Anyway, she called Mum in to deliver the news that I was being moved down in every single set, away from Billie, Steph, Sophie, Stace and Gemma – we were being separated in every class except PE.

I went mad when my mum sat me down to tell me. I properly lost it and remember screaming: 'They can shove it. I literally don't care! I am just going to carry on going to all my normal classes. I'm not moving, they'll have to chuck me out! I don't know anyone in the lower classes! What about my friends?'

There were tears and tantrums galore, but in the end, down I went. To be honest, nothing really changed. I just caused mischief in the new class and our original crowd of six got even bigger as I brought all the naughty, cool girls into our group. If I look back now, I can totally see why they did it – I was disrupting top sets full of bright and switched-on girls who were cleverer than me and weren't coming to school to be entertained by me – but at the time it was the end of the world.

I also remember once going to Spain to visit Billie and her younger sister Sam when they lived out there and looking around the gift shop before we flew home. I was always the one who would go for the weird gift or souvenir to bring back, and I spotted a pencil case that was an actual metal bus with wheels that you could push along. It made me laugh a lot and I decided it would be perfect for class.

So, first day back after the holidays and I was sitting

there at the back (as usual) and everyone had already seen the comedy pencil case and they all knew where I was going with it. The first class back was maths with my favourite teacher I liked to wind up. At the front, one of my mates shouted: 'Hey, Ferne, can I borrow your rubber?'

I replied: 'Sure, hang on a minute, I'll just pass it down.' With that, I put the bus on the floor and pushed it straight down to the front of the classroom, to the desk of the person wanting the rubber. She used it, put it back inside and pushed the bus back up the classroom. The whole class was in hysterics, except the teacher, of course, as the lesson was in chaos.

There was another time, when *Big Brother* first started, that I became obsessed with Pete Burns. I have no idea why. One day in class I refused to answer to my name and would only respond if the science teacher would call me Pete Burns. I stuck to it all lesson and, in the end, she just gave in and started calling me Pete.

My imagination hadn't gone away and art was definitely my favourite subject (I went on to do it for A level.) I was in every play that the school put on and, despite not being top of the class for English, I had no trouble learning my lines (despite my mum's worry I wouldn't remember the words). I absolutely loved performing.

Even now when I am distracted or getting ready for something, I will break out into song or a little shoulder shimmy. I love a good singalong or a bit of role play.

I used to do impressions all the time and I suppose around this time I started to really play up to the 'class clown' label. (In fact, I won the award for class clown in 2006.) It rubbed off on my friends too – what a lot of *TOWIE* fans don't know is that Billie has a wicked sense of humour and, at times, is worse than me. It's hilarious for me to see how much Nelly has inherited that, and I can't wait to see the comedy she brings Billie and Greg. It's that thing where, looking back to when you were a teenager, you realise you literally used to waste hours doing nothing, hanging around the house and causing aggravation. Basically, that's what Billie and I did – spend time at my house when my mum was at work and cause chaos, pranking any victim we could find.

I think maybe because my parents were splitting up, they cut me some more slack than they might usually, but to be honest, all our mums were cool about us hanging around together.

One day, before we moved out of our family house, I bought some cigarettes aged thirteen (actually, I think Billie might have 'borrowed' them from her mum Sue,

I'm not sure, or else I did that thing of buying one cigarette for 50p in the playground) and me and Billie
smoked them in my mum's bedroom. Obviously that
wasn't a great idea – my parents aren't smokers and I had
no idea how much one cigarette would smoke the whole
place out. We crept into their en suite, closed all the
doors, but thought it would be fine as we could keep all
the smoke in the bedroom and then blow it out the
window. It just went everywhere. It was so bad that my
sister (who was looking after us) stormed up the stairs
and went mental.

In fact, a lot of the scrapes I got into with Billie seemed
to involve the window in my parents' bedroom. It looked
out on to an alleyway and during our last summer there,
I remember my dad hiring a tree cutter to come and cut
down all the branches that were blocking the sunlight.
Anyway, this tree cutter rocked up one morning ready to
start work – with his wife and kids in tow, which just
seemed odd but meant a lot of fun for Billie and me. Off
my mum and dad went, leaving my sister in charge. We
were given strict instructions to be polite, to offer him
tea, coffee, biscuits, but to leave him alone to get on with
his work – he didn't need us hanging around and getting
in his way.

It turned out what he needed less was what happened when we decided to pop our heads out of the window every five minutes to see if he was okay. We would open the window, lean right out and shout: 'You all right? How's it going? Need anything up that ladder?' The trouble with Billie and me is that we don't know when to pack it in, and that harmless shouting out of the window stopped having an impact so we had to think of something even more annoying.

We decided to get a toilet roll, tear long bits of paper off, soak them in water and lob them out of the window straight at this poor bloke's head – as he was balancing in a tree harness, holding a moving chainsaw. I still remember us wetting ourselves as the tissue would smack the side of his head with a *thwack!* and how the paper would cling to the side of his face, the water acting like some kind of glue that kept it there until he would pull it off from the side of his cheek and throw it to the ground. We would chuck it, hear the noise of the impact and duck down before he had a chance to turn his body around in his harness. We heard him shout: 'They're bloody chucking things at me now.' It seemed like hours of fun – until he knocked on the door to grass us up.

We were worse with neighbours, though. We had this

poor family who lived across from us and we *tormented* them. They were just a normal couple who lived there with their three children. I suppose if I am honest they were quite a square family and were easy targets, really. They had a daughter called Mary, the fact she was two years older than us made it all the more fun.

My bedroom was opposite hers and we would hide in wait there, plotting until she went up to her room. We would see her there, playing with her toys, open my window and scream 'MARYYYYYYYY' at the top of our voices, drawing out the 'y' at the end so it sounded as if the house was on fire. In fact, if you imagine it like Ant and Dec say 'I'm a celebrity . . . Get me out of here!' at the start of the show, with that echo, you have a good idea. Anyway, this wasn't the Australian jungle, it was a cul de sac with fifteen houses in Brentwood, so it sounded as if something was mega wrong. We would scream and Mary would rush to her window, her head spinning around as she tried to work out where the shouting was coming from, and we would duck down, pissing ourselves. In the end, Mary's dad came round and that was the end of that. Mum would come up and tell us to pack it in and we used to look at her, bewildered, and deny it all, asking: 'Why would we waste our time doing that?'

We were also monster prank callers. Anyone would do, even parents of our friends. We would call up, putting the phone right to our mouths, and just chew chocolate down the phone really noisily. If we could find a victim, they were ours and that included teachers too, though the one time I got internally suspended for swearing I was gutted. It was one thing pranking but another thing to be rude and disrespectful to a teacher. I was always brought up to be polite and that was a step too far, even for me.

Not content with pranking strangers, I used to drag my mum into my mad make-believe world, often causing maximum embarrassment as she is the opposite to me – she is mega, mega shy. I used to get Mum to drive me to Bluewater so we could check out the clothes in River Island and Warehouse. On the way I would sit in the back singing along to Craig David on the radio, complete with the dance moves even though I was sitting down and strapped in. I would soon get bored and start to play 'the game'. Poor Mum, she has lived so many years with my mad ways, and she never knew what was coming next. My favourite would be to make up these situations – dramas, really, a bit like a mini episode of *EastEnders* – and she would get the worst role that involved proper crying or a lot of shouting. (If we were stuck in traffic on the motorway she used to want to die.)

But me being me, I couldn't just leave it there – I had to push it to the limit. So we would get to Bluewater, park the car and hit the shops, and all of a sudden I would go for it. We would be in John Lewis and Mum would be looking at the shoes or trying stuff on and I would suddenly pipe up (using my best posh voice) in her direction: 'Oh Dotty dahhrling, do take a look at this coat. Isn't it divine? It is *so* you. Do try it on.'

Mum would be dying inside but would have to play along: that was the rule – you couldn't break out of character or it got worse for you. I would be hiding behind the changing room curtain wetting myself and Mum would be styling it out like a pro. I never stopped finding it hilarious. I reckon if you asked my mum to sum me up in a few words she would say: exhausting, loving, loyal, tricky, but in John Lewis when I made her 'do Dotty' I'm sure there would have been swearing involved.

Though I hated moving into our new house, it was weirdly one of the most fun times of my childhood – it was when we started experimenting with drinking and smoking and generally just street-raking around the place. It was new territory for us: Brentwood was our stomping ground but here we were in Shenfield and no one knew who we were. Because of the break-up, my mum was so laid-back about everything and I got away with murder, to be honest, and I totally milked the situation to my advantage. The gang would all pile round mine, we would climb out of my bedroom window and smoke on this flat roof that stuck out just below my window ledge. It was big enough for all of us and we would sit out in whatever weather, puffing away. It was the stuff of teen-age dreams – a smoking shelter, a side alleyway for easy access, and a corner shop where no one asked any questions and we gave no answers, so we could buy as many fags as we wanted.

If ever there is a dare or something needs to be done, I'm there doing it, no questions asked, no drama. I will give anything a go once and really believe that you shouldn't say 'I can't' until you've tried. I had the massive advantage of never feeling stressed about getting caught (or I would feel the fear and do it anyway). It makes sense, then, why the group always picked me as the one to go and get the fags from the corner shop. I had a deep voice that I used to put on – we all decided it made me sound really mature (at least twenty-one), and I would practise it with the girls to make sure I had it spot on. All psyched up, I would then go in and do the deed while the rest of them waited round the side of the alleyway for me to come back with the goods.

There was one time that stands out, when I massively over-delivered on my fag run performance. I went in as usual and asked for my normal stash of Marlboro Lights, and there and then I decided to go for the double whammy and try for some vodka too. I just had the guy behind the till eating out of my hand, I could tell. He was totally believing that I was the right age and not even looking at me to try to work out how old I really was. Now was the time to smash it. My 'cigarette look' was particularly strong that day – I had my sister's glasses on and her ID, and my hair was slicked right back to look super-sophisticated. It's funny now the lengths girls go to in order to look older than they are – often they get it so wrong by thinking the shorter the skirt the better. In my day, the name of the game was to cover up and look relaxed. Back then we dressed like our mums – it was all calf-length skirts and buttoned-up shirts.

So there I was, asking for twenty fags, when I casually added in: 'Oh, almost forgot the vodka,' as I put the bottle on the counter for the assistant to scan through. He didn't even give me a second glance, so it was mission accomplished for me and happy days for all of us. I was wearing a long coat with deep pockets on each side, perfect for stashing the supplies just in case I bumped into any adults on the way back. I put the booze in one pocket, the cigs in another, and ran back to meet the gang. As I approached them, I put a hand in each pocket and whipped out both the bottle and the fags. They couldn't believe their eyes.

It's weird when you're young and you have such a tight friendship unit, they become the most important people to you and set up for life a pattern of fierce female friendships. But I look back now and realise I didn't always extend that love and kindness to my mum – it was a classic case of taking things out on those closest to you, I suppose. You could argue I felt secure enough to show her my worst side, but whatever the reason, it wasn't my best work. Once we were all settled and the divorce came through, Mum started seeing someone, and my teenage self made it very clear I wasn't okay with this new relationship. Like every teenager, I was selfish, only bothered about myself and wanting her there 100 per cent just for me – I didn't want to share her with anyone else and I made her feel guilty all the time. I feel so bad when I look back now. I suppose I also feel bad about my sister too. I think because I was younger I really struggled, I took up all the airtime and everyone just assumed Sophie was coping fine with it all, especially as she acted so grown up. I only realised that wasn't the case one New Year's Eve when she burst into tears about everything. I think then my mum realised she was hurting too.

The truth is that most people don't like change, especially not kids, and I was no exception. My dad moved to Devon, he was six hours away, and that made me feel as if a lifetime of closeness had been lost. It felt as though it was all slipping through my fingers and I didn't know how to process it. The thing is, when I was bad it didn't make me feel good: I would apologise straight away and couldn't get over it until I knew I'd been forgiven. But this situation was out of my control and I couldn't make it go away.

Doing a book like this means you have to really look at yourself and I won't lie, that's been hard, but I'm very aware of my flaws and I've never pretended to be anything I'm not. I know I have always really enjoyed being the centre of attention; it's been part of my personality from a young age. I also know that, sometimes, I behave in ways that make it hard for the people I love to like me and have my back. I can be my own worst enemy, but I also know the people closest to me would seriously say that I don't have a bad bone in my body.

My mum is a qualified sports therapist and works from home – she has a special treatment room in the house that she uses for her clients. When I was much younger, if I'd been particularly mean to her, I would go up to my room and write these long notes saying: 'I'm sorry, Mummy. I love you so much and I know I am terrible. I promise I won't do it again,' and then list all the things I was sorry for. I would creep down the stairs and push the notes under the door. Mum would read them and keep them on the side (she still has them now). She never said much about them but I hoped that she understood why I behaved the way I did. I don't know what I would do without my mum – she is my best friend and I've always known that, even when I didn't show it.

4

The Teen Years

Glamour is everywhere in Essex and a night out on the town is a big deal, especially when you are underage. I will never forget the excitement when we started hitting the clubs and getting our faces on the scene. We started so young that now when I go out with my mates, people must look at us and think we're about a hundred since we've been out and about for years. Billie and me look back at photos of ourselves from the time and we get hysterical – how the hell could any boys have fancied us looking like that? Some of the outfits and haircuts were truly criminal but we thought we were amazing!

We first started going out when we were about fifteen

and we would go to Chelmsford, all dressed up and full of worry about what would happen if we didn't get in – the fear was real.

When it came to blagging our way into places, we smashed it every single time. We never, ever got turned away and we were always so proud not to have to do the walk of shame away from the club door as the whole queue watched. We would either get lifts (imagine being dropped at the nightclub door by your mum, but we styled it out!) or get a cab.

We had a little routine as we drove to wherever we were going – it was like the team talk before a match. I was the hyper-upper in the car, the one who used to run through all the scenarios we might encounter, all the possible pitfalls. I would go through the checklist of questions that the bouncers might ask to trip us up and got everyone to rehearse their answers until they were word perfect. I would say: 'Right, guys, what are we celebrating tonight? Are we out for a birthday or exams? What star sign are you? What year were you born? What hospital were you born in?' We always had a Plan B – you name it, there wasn't a single situation I hadn't thought of that would block us from getting in.

When we first started going out we were obsessed with

the One Three One nightclub in Romford (mainly as it was so easy to get into). We would get the train, walk out of Romford station and the club was right there on the left – perfect for those of us too young to drive. Talk about having it all right on your doorstep. The place would be heaving with teenagers, as it was well known as the place you could always get in without many questions asked. We had our firm favourites once we moved on from our street-raking days round my way, or in Ongar, where Sam and Billie lived; our taste got much more sophisticated and we started going to places like the Tas bar (another place we had no worries getting served). This was like the practice run, when we were aged around fourteen, fifteen, before we moved on to the clubs and bars – and boys.

We tackled getting into the clubs in the same planned way we had tried the pubs and bars – the key is to *always* have your story straight and be able to think on your feet. Sugar Hut was never a problem when it came to being let in – we even managed to get into the little gallery room that was always full of older and more sophisticated clubbers. Again, back then, we were always on a mission to dress really old – seriously, we looked so weird and actually like pensioners on some of our big nights out. The bigger the club, the more middle-aged we dressed. Such bizarre logic when I think back.

I look at some of the pictures from those days and it's hilarious. Sam would be wearing a leather skirt (so far so normal), but then on the top half would have put it with a buttoned shirt and a blazer (basically like she was going to a job interview). I would have on a corset (again, fine) but would wear it with office-like trousers or I would go for a mid-calf-length dress and kitten heels. It's funny really, because everyone thinks that all Essex girls are the same, that we go out wearing hardly any clothes, walking around in heels so high we can't stand up straight, with our boobs spilling out everywhere, but we didn't really ever do that. Don't get me wrong, obviously plenty of people do – I know because I see them out and about, and each to their own. But we mostly looked like we were there for work experience! I suppose we were just always so confident as a group – swagger gets you in, lots of eye contact and some friendly banter, and we all had plenty of that. When Sam and Billie moved to Spain we really got a taste for the clubbing scene as it was so relaxed out there – they'd let us in and give us loads of booze; we didn't even need our ID (just as well as mine belonged to my sister and Billie borrowed hers from a friend).

It's funny: I suppose I'm coming across as mega confident, but I've always been able to put a positive spin on everything. The fact is that at that age, when we started going out and getting noticed by boys, I did have lots of insecurities about how I looked. It didn't help that the boys at school used to call me 'Goose' because my nose reminded them of a beak. Now, let's be honest, there is nothing nice about geese – they don't even sound good, they honk! It wasn't as though they were comparing me to a nice fluffy duck or an elegant swan. I was massively insecure – I knew all my friends were gorgeous and there I was with this nose and I was also so much taller than all the boys my age. It didn't do a lot for my confidence at all, but I didn't show that side to many people.

When we were out we used to play this hilarious game we made up called 'Will You Get with My Mate?' I look back now and *cringe* because that was basically the game – we would be out in a club, turn around to a group of boys, strangers, and say: 'Will you get with my mate?' And then one of us would kiss them and we'd move on to the next one – imagine! We used to rake around clubs in our posse and look for random boys to play the game with. We'd have competitions and I took it very seriously – I used to always win.

As we got older we took it up a gear and started to get into Sam's in Brentwood on their under-eighteens night where we would listen to garage. We also used to love Zeus and Dukes in Chelmsford – I will never forget how grown up I used to feel as we all stood around in the club, smoking and looking out for good-looking boys. It seems so mental to also remember there was no social media back then, or even much text messaging – it was all MSN or MySpace and I was always talking to some boy; I liked to make sure I had a few possible ones on the go.

This was about the time that boys properly made an appearance in my life, and one in particular was firmly in my sights: Lewis F. As we go on in this book you will see a pattern: when I like someone they are automatically 'the one' and I become obsessed, which doesn't always work to my advantage. I invest all my time in the person I like and I just make it really clear how I feel. I've never been one to play it cool (maybe I should learn a lesson from that, but I just can't help it – if I like someone, I like them, and I expect them to make it clear they like me back if they feel the same). *What* is the point of games? I have genuinely never understood it because it just isn't what I'm like. One thing you will learn from this book is that I wear my heart on my sleeve. But I think this attitude was a bit too much for Lewis – he didn't quite know how to handle me when I made it clear how much I liked him.

I thought Lewis was everything. To me he was the perfect boy: I would think about him all day and then get home from school and spend all night talking to him on the phone. (I think back and wonder when anyone else in my house ever actually got to use the phone – it was glued to my ear.) I used to live for those phone calls, even though we didn't really have a lot to say to each other – it was just the fact he was choosing to be on the phone to me that made me so happy. I sometimes see him around now, and it makes me smile to think how properly mental about him I was back when we were young. All he did was kick about the place, but he was my ultimate guy. Looking back it makes me smile at how innocent it all was, so playground, but it felt like the biggest thing ever.

A lot of girls I knew were experimenting with sex, but I was the absolute opposite. I was such a good girl really (though I did have one little fumble that got round the school – I made sure I denied it as it was really embarrassing). In truth, I was probably a bit frigid at school in comparison to other girls, but that didn't stop me obsessing. I never judged: every girl has their sexual learning curve, mine just came later. I suppose admitting that I didn't know what to do scared me. I was paranoid that people would get to hear I was no good at it and didn't know what was what – at that age you're so worried about seeming to know the answers to everything. That's definitely something I would love to be able to say to my younger self: it is totally fine to admit you don't know everything and it's okay to be upfront about it. In fact, people will probably respect you more. That's all part of growing up and finding out who you are. I could never have called Lewis my boyfriend, although I convinced myself I loved him – but, alas, he didn't want to commit. (The comedy – we were fifteen!) The final straw was when he flirted with my friend's little sister – I was heartbroken.

I think the other reason I wasn't jumping in and out bed with people was because, unlike a lot of my friends, I had a Saturday job. Throughout life I have never had a game plan, and sometimes that has been difficult as I've drifted a bit. I certainly had no idea that if you were good at something you could make it your career. Looking back, there have been a few things I did really well at that I could have taken further, like netball, which I've always loved, but I suppose I lacked the confidence. But when I was fourteen, I decided I wanted to do something that was just mine. I can't really remember why I got the job; it wasn't that we needed the money or my parents were worried about me getting up to no good. I think I just wanted some independence and my own money – all that socialising was pricey and the clothes and stuff on top meant that it was easier if I had my own money.

After the bottom fell out of the trading market for my dad, he started working in recruitment back in Brentwood and got talking with his friend Nigel, who owned a local salon. Dad asked him to interview me and I got the job to work there on Saturdays and one late-night Thursday a month. It was genuinely the best job. I had the most amazing time and loved every minute of it. It made me feel so grown up and in control of my own life and I threw myself right into it with everything. I seriously learned how to clean mirrors like a demon: there is no one who can shine a mirror as well as me – never a smear in sight! I shampooed people's hair, swept the floors, restocked all the shampoo and conditioners, sorted the magazines and made all the tea and coffee. I was sent on the lunch runs every single week and I can still remember the order my boss would give me: three chicken strips, two whole pieces of chicken, chips and Diet Coke. The owner of the salon was also a local councillor and as part of my work duty I would go around and knock on people's doors with leaflets canvassing for him.

I definitely brought my joker personality to the salon floor, and I think they all liked having me around. I love people, so it was the perfect job for me: the salon was always full of different sorts of people and I found it fascinating to find out all about them. As I said earlier, I think that's also one of the things I loved most about my time in the jungle too. I've always been interested in other people's stories, their journey and hearing different opinions on stuff. I love to ask a question and I would listen to the customers as they told me their problems, and I would happily offer advice and join in – I really was in my element. I loved entertaining everyone too. I would do impressions and invent Dizzee Rascal raps that I would perform on the salon floor. I had this thing they called my 'mad half an hour', where at the end of a shift I would break into song, do a dance and just generally let off steam. It became something they associated with the end of the day and it was a real feel-good moment. I worked in that salon until I was eighteen and I truly loved every minute of it. I learned so much but I was adamant that I didn't want to be hairdresser – I'm not sure why, but I didn't long to do it for a living. I did love the money, though. From the age of fourteen I had £25 every Saturday; when I turned eighteen it went up to £40. (I don't think my boss was happy about that!)

The customers were great but so were the rest of the staff. Everyone who worked there was older than me and we would go out for the night in a big group. It was different from a night on the town with my schoolmates: my hairdressing colleagues went to different places and seemed very sophisticated in comparison. I relished the fact that I had something separate from school and my family – it really did make me feel grown up and I think it helped me be less angry about the divorce. It was good to feel good at something.

Like all great things, it came to an end with the realisation that I didn't want to be a Saturday girl for ever and I stopped working there when school got serious. I did my GCSEs and did well enough to make sure I could stay on and do my A levels. I picked Art, Theatre Studies and Media Studies and felt happy to have the security of doing them at school. Despite my disruptive behaviour lower down in the school, I really did love that place and was so happy that Billie and the gang were staying on too. Sam decided to leave at sixteen and got a job in a local bank. In a way, because I didn't know what I wanted to do, I was relieved I now had another two years at school before I needed to make any big decisions – it meant more time for fun and going out.

But I suppose this would be a good time to introduce Tony, the guy who came into my world and tipped it upside down.

5

Don't You Blue-tick Me

All around me people were making big life-changing decisions and all I could think about was Tony. It's weird, because when he first came into my life I remember being massively underwhelmed by him – he really wasn't my type. But although he went on to become known as my Mr Heartbreak after everything that happened, I'm so glad he was my learning curve. My time with Tony taught me so much about myself, how I should be treated and about how relationships should work. So, although it didn't feel like it at the time, it was a great learning experience.

I suppose your teens are for drama. It's almost the law that you experience high-level boy pain, that you think your heart will never heal and that you will never love another like your first crush. Some might say I never grew out of my dramatic stage (!) but, trust me, my feelings for Tony ran deep and they were the real deal. My whole existence revolved around him, much to my mum's dismay, but the worst thing you can say to anyone experiencing young heartbreak is that they'll get over it. My pet hate was always when people used to tell me: 'You will look back at this in years to come and laugh.' I would think: I doubt it – what will *ever* be funny about this in the future when I'm not exactly laughing right now? But actually I look back and (as well as cringing at some of the scenarios) I do laugh at some of the things that went on, but when you're in it you never think you will be out of it. My God, I was infatuated with the boy and he just had me on a string.

I met him through Mark Wright and his group of mates. Sam had started talking to Mark on MySpace at the time and we used to hang around the Slug and Lettuce or Sugar Hut on Brentwood High Street. (Funnily enough, my mate Jerry met her now husband at the same time I met Tony, so at least it worked out for one of us.) We were right in the thick of being out all the time. We would rampage about the place thinking we were it – we were everywhere and making sure people knew who we were.

Back in the day, the thing was very much MySpace, that's how we all communicated – but I don't know how we ever made any actual arrangements without the iPhone and the million ways we now have to stay in touch. When I think about how my phone is glued to my hand at all times, I can't imagine my world without being in constant touch with my mates. Never mind how social media lets you know what's going on and where everyone is at all times. It is dangerous really, but so addictive. Back then there was none of that.

Anyway, the night I met Tony we were all out as a group of girls in the Slug and Lettuce. Sam and Jerry were having a little stalk, as we always used to go round the pub in pairs to check out who was there and what the vibe was. Someone came in and said that Mark Wright was outside in his car and wanted to talk to Sam – classic Essex boy behaviour, summoning you over so that he can try and put it on you in front of his mates and look the big I am. Sam wanted me to go outside with her, but I didn't fancy being in the way of them getting with each other so I said I would stay inside and wait for her. Off she went and a few minutes later she called me from one of their mobile phones to tell me to come outside. So out I went and got into the car. I was sixteen and so sure of myself, no nerves, just loads of typical sixteen-year-old front.

I climbed into the car and turned to Tony and said: 'Is this your car?' He told me it was and I said something really sarcastic like: 'Yeah, right, your mum's car more like.' Tony was in the front and I could tell he thought I was out of order but also quite loved it too. I didn't fancy him immediately. He wasn't really my usual type – not a classic Essex boy. He was almost Spanish-like with dark, slicked-back hair (but he was really tanned like the Essex crowd). He was a good-looking boy but, to be honest, my first impression was that he was a bit goony-looking. We chatted for a bit, went back inside and started hanging around together as a group from then on, really. We all went to places like the Essex polo and Nu bar, and spent time going round Mark and Tony's houses, hanging out and lying on sofas not doing a lot, as you do when you're that age.

At the time I was a virgin and once, when I was round at the Wright house, Mark's brother Josh, Tony and someone else all asked me how many boys I'd slept with. I was mortified. To me the very worst thing I could say was that I hadn't slept with anyone. So I decided to make myself look ridiculously experienced and said that I had already slept with two boys. Thinking back, it's so embarrassing – two blokes on the bedpost at sixteen, not exactly the classiest image to give, was it? Girls, trust me, if there's one thing I've learned it's that telling the truth about being a virgin is totally the way forward – there is absolutely zero shame in holding on to it until the time is right. I didn't understand that it was more embarrassing to make out that I'd been jumping in and out of bed with boys when I was so young – it certainly didn't make them think any better of me (if they believed me at all!).

Tony was twenty-one and the most mature and sophisticated guy I'd ever met: he had a car, was older and had cash to be flash, plus we had a shared interest in music. We soon found out that we loved the same bands and songs – from the very beginning, he understood and loved my quirky, non-typical-Essex-girl ways. We got on well from the get-go, but our first date was a disaster. He didn't really plan anything special. (That didn't change during the whole time we were together. I don't think he ever really put any thought into being massively romantic or arranging anything nice – whatever we did was always so random.) He came to the house and picked me up in his Golf and we decided to go to see a Nicolas Cage film (something so boring that I can't even remember what it was called). It was dire, and we'd only watched fifteen minutes before I turned to Tony and said I thought it was rubbish and we should leave. That was it, our first date: we left the crap film and drove around for a bit in his car before he dropped me home. We didn't even go for dinner.

We did have a laugh though, and chatted non-stop. I remember being surprised that I could have such a good time with someone I didn't actually fancy. That was that, really – we just started hanging around with each other. I remember it wasn't hard work at the beginning. He would always message me and arrange a time to meet – there were no games at all, but nothing was ever made official either. We fell into a pattern where I would go round his house and we were sort of together. I can't even properly remember the first time I slept with him, but we had been dating a long while before I did the deed with him.

As I think back for this book, it makes me realise it wasn't actually love, more an infatuation on my part, but it felt incredibly dramatic and real at the time. A lot of what happened with Tony is a blur because it was so off and on (and when it was on, it was never really 100 per cent on). Anyway, this first 'on' period lasted a few weeks until I went on my first girly holiday to Magaluf. We'd just had a few snogs at this point, but I was really starting to fall for him. It was that time between year 11 and year 12, when we were finally allowed to go away as a group of girls on our own, abroad for the first time. It was so exciting it was all I could think about. But I was also anxious as, although I'd been saving up all my Saturday money and my mum had kindly given me some cash towards the holiday, I wasn't sure how much I would need. I'd never been away without my parents there to pay for meals and stuff and had no idea how expensive Spain would be.

We were driving along in Tony's car one day and he asked me what was wrong. I told him that I was worried about the holiday and having enough cash for spending money, as I didn't know how much the other girls were taking. He was dropping me home and all of a sudden he pulled over and jumped out, saying he had to run an errand. He got back in and handed me £200, looked at me and said: 'I really just want you to have a good time out there and not worry. Take it.'

Off I went to have the most fantastic break. But by the

time I came home from Spain, things had fizzled out – there was no fallout, it was just that he was busy and so was I. I didn't really see him out and about, and then I got caught up in the most amazing summer where I met Alfie, the fittest boy I had ever seen. I watched him dancing in a nightclub and that was it, I was smitten. Tony seemed like a distant memory, though he was to become a recurring presence over the next two years. But during that summer it was all about Alfie. I was warned he was a bit of a player but I was head over heels. That was also the summer that Sam and I started hanging around together a lot more, as Billie had a boyfriend and was all loved up, but for Sam and me it was the summer of fun. I decided that Alfie was going to be 'the one' and set my plan in motion. One weekend my mum was away and Sam and me were staying at mine. After a night out I invited a few people back and that was the night I lost my virginity.

I think most girls will identify with the fact that, often, the first time is a very complicated moment – it is rare that the earth moves! But in typical Ferne fashion, mine was less complicated and more comedy. I didn't have much experience, but in my opinion Alfie seemed to be a bit of a vain boy and was paranoid about some spots he had on his face. As we were getting comfortable he asked me if I had a clove of garlic, as he'd heard that it helped with spots, so off I went and returned with a peeled clove to hand him. (I had no idea how he thought it would help his skin, I won't lie, I was worried.) He took the garlic and rubbed the clove all over his face. So I ended up making out in a room that stank of garlic as we listened to Paolo Nutini's 'Loving You'. Talk about living the dream!

In the middle of the night I ran into my sister's room, where Sam was sleeping, and I whispered: 'I've done it!' and we hugged. I was the last member of the group to lose her virginity.

It wasn't exactly a Cinderella moment as, a few weeks later, he ended up getting with another girl and that was the end of that, really. The final straw was the next day when I found a dried-up bit of garlic on my bedside table. He hadn't even thrown it away – what a memento.

Despite how I could be about boys I liked, I genuinely wasn't sad about Alfie, maybe because sleeping with him hadn't been the great *Romeo and Juliet* moment I thought it would be. As the summer of fun continued, Sam and me hit the clubs hard and we started going to London. There was one night that had been organised

FERNE McCANN

by two brothers who were friends of ours and they invited us down. Now, do not ask me why, but we decided to go in fancy dress, even though that wasn't the dress code. We got on the train at Brentwood wearing tutus and these hilarious skinny rib cardigans with little collars and sequined tigers on the back from Topshop. I don't know what we thought we looked like getting off the train at Liverpool Street station dressed like a pair of lunatics in tutus and sparkly cardigans. We had a great night and I ended up going back to one of the guy's houses for a few drinks and a bit of an after party. This boy ended up being the second person I slept with. I was still naïve and inexperienced and I didn't realise you had to wait for a certain order of events when it came to the male anatomy in that situation, another learning curve!

When I think back on my young self it makes me cringe, but at the time, it's how you learn, isn't it? We all start from the same place and that's the thing I learned, it isn't a competition, it really is best to be kind to yourself and not feel any peer pressure. We are all at different stages at different times and that is totally fine. Anyway, we slept together and that was that. We saw each other around Essex and were friends – all good, until it came

66

back to haunt me a few months later when I got back with Tony.

After the mad summer, we went back to sixth form and started going out at the weekends, which meant I'd bump into Tony again. We started talking and then things got serious quite quickly. It felt very real almost straight away. I'd never been in love before and I fell hard – my feelings were overwhelming and too much for my young self to handle. But little did I know that my tutu night would come back to haunt me a few months later.

It is hard to explain how incestuous Essex is – sometimes it feels like you cannot blink without someone passing it on. People are talking about what you've done before you've even done it. My tutu night is a classic example of that as the boy I slept with decided to tell Tony what had happened, why I don't know. I later found out that the boy worked with Tony and our night together became nothing more than office gossip. At the time I didn't know any of this, all I knew was that one day Tony just stopped calling me. It is one of the worst things that can happen to a girl and I was heartbroken. It was so bad that I told my mum all about it, which obviously meant I had to tell her I'd slept with that boy – I must have been distraught! I even got her to ring Tony for me, I was so desperate to keep him.

Eventually we slipped back into the old patterns of local dates at places like La Tasca on the high street – it was never planned or a big deal; it was comfortable. We didn't really act like a couple dating. (Although he did take me to see *Dirty Dancing* the musical once.) I couldn't seem to do anything to this guy to make it go official. He just wanted to keep it casual whilst never fully letting me go. I would have done anything to be his girlfriend. I think I was just too young to understand that some people will play games in order to get the upper hand; you learn that with age and experience, I guess. It never occurred to me to question his behaviour, because I loved him so much. Tony could do no wrong in my eyes.

I found a black false nail in his bed once, and I asked him: 'What's this?' He said it belonged to his mum and she must have left it there when she was changing the sheets. I think if I look back without my blinkers on, I can see it was the classic scenario of young girl goes out with older guy who isn't as into her as she is into him, and young girl is prepared to put up with anything, which means that older guy does what he wants. Certainly from my point of view, things became very tricky, though I totally take my share of the responsibility: I was very needy, and the more I wanted him the more it must have driven him mad. I know I made it seem as though I would put up with anything he threw at me, and it felt as if he pushed the boundaries as far as he could. You can't blame the guy, in a way. I put up with it and he pushed it more, and so the cycle continued.

But it is hard for someone to respect you when you don't respect yourself. It was just a very toxic relationship. He would come round for the night and just as we were settling in, he would get a text from the boys at Nu bar, so he would go off and meet them, say he was coming back, but I wouldn't see him again that night.

I was lying one time in bed with my mum and feeling really down about the whole situation, partly because I knew it was also my fault, and a text pinged through from him saying 'I love you'. I didn't know what to make of it, because it was so out of character but obviously it was what I wanted to hear. I later found out he sent it because he didn't fancy her and being there had made him realise that he couldn't stop thinking of me on a date with another girl. For me that one line cancelled out the date. 'I couldn't stop thinking about you' was everything I wanted to hear and more. Looking back, I actually think he sent me mad, but then I acted mad too. I think that in his eyes he wasn't doing anything wrong, as we were never actually officially boyfriend and girlfriend. He told me as far as he was concerned he never wanted to label it like that.

I asked my mum afterwards: 'Why didn't you tell me I was being so insane?' She said there had never been any point telling me what I didn't want to hear, as I did what I wanted to anyway (sounds about right.) I am almost embarrassed that you are reading some of the things I did – like ringing him all night, non-stop, and not taking the hint when he just wouldn't answer. I would leave so many messages clogging up his mailbox and sometimes would cry down the phone like a mentalist, but nothing could make him call me back if he didn't want to.

I feel so sorry for my younger self – but I just couldn't see straight. I used to buy dresses hoping that he'd think I'd made a huge effort for him. I would go out to the same places 'accidentally' and spend the whole night keeping an eye on whichever girl he was talking to, trying to work out if he fancied them. I would lurk around the club following him, and then be one of the last to leave, hoping he would want me to go home with him. It wasn't that I was falling more in love with him, I was just becoming obsessed with what he was doing when he wasn't with me and all I wanted was for him to love me back.

I tried to take control of the on–off situation by deciding to go on dates. But he was there in the back of my mind, and the thought of him stopped me doing a lot of things. That's the other thing they don't tell you: what you think is your whole world when you're a teenager isn't remotely relevant later in life. It really is a moment, and not what ends up defining you. It is so dangerous to make someone the centre of your world at a time when you have to make such important decisions. They may sound like wise words now, but back then I didn't have a clue. It makes me appreciate my mum so much when I look back – I want to shake my young self, so God knows how she felt.

I made a lot of stupid decisions. I wanted to go to drama school after my A levels but I didn't want to leave him so I didn't go – I thought that if I wasn't in Essex he wouldn't be interested. All my decisions were based around him. I even booked a holiday in Marbella at the same time as him and the boys so that I would be 'around'. I would turn up at the same events as him and we'd end up going home together, and in my own mad world that made me feel loved. It was very screwed up, really.

His silences drove me mad. One morning I got in the car and drove round to his house because he hadn't answered his phone all night. He lived with his mum and dad and I screeched round, pulling on to his driveway. I jumped out and started to pound on his front door. When I got no answer from the front, I ran round into the garden and started banging on his back door. I was sobbing: 'Why do you *do* this to me?' God knows what the neighbours and his parents made of it. I wasn't exactly showing myself in the greatest light, but he consumed me and I couldn't control my seventeen-year-old infatuated behaviour.

He would ignore me and then love-bomb me. Perhaps he didn't really know what he wanted but, to my mind, it was the cruellest way to behave towards me – giving me a glimmer of hope and then snatching it away. Once he said: 'I want to make this official. I want you to be by my side as my girlfriend.' Then immediately after, he would go for days on end without calling or texting. I would get fed up and go out on the town to drown my sorrows, and there he would be. We'd go home together and so the cycle would carry on. It wasn't healthy for either of us and not sustainable, but I knew I wouldn't be strong enough to end it. In the end he did it for both of us. I suppose I was expecting 'the chat' when he came round carrying a box of my stuff (subtle!). He just came in and said what we had both been thinking – that it couldn't go on the way it had been and he should probably be single for a while. I was heartbroken.

I know it sounds bad but, looking back, I can't blame him 100 per cent for the way it was. I know now that so much of our 'relationship' was me wanting it to mean so much more to him. Those feelings didn't really stop even when he broke up with me and started seeing someone else. I would get drunk and message him, even if he was with another girl. I am ashamed to say that only really stopped when the girl he was seeing texted me back: 'You have got to stop this, it is embarrassing, Ferne.'

I just had to accept it in the end. You do get to that point eventually, don't you? Something just clicks and in my case pride did kick in (with a helping hand from Tony after he deleted me from Facebook). Once he cut me off I had to deal with the whole situation and accept that my feelings for him weren't reciprocated. I got really low but suddenly, like a bolt of lightning, it came to me that lying in bed watching back to back *Gossip Girl* wasn't going to cure my broken heart. So when a friend suggested that I join her travelling, I jumped at the chance. I'm amazed Mum let me go as I was only eighteen, but I think it was clear to everyone that the best thing was for me to get away from Tony, Essex and everything. I was embarrassed and heartbroken but he was a young boy who probably didn't want a long-term girlfriend and I had to get on with my life. No one was going to do that for me but me.

Going travelling was liberating and the very best medicine, like a spring clean. We went to Vietnam, Singapore and Thailand and had the best time. I decided I could do better than Tony. I cleared my Facebook page of all my old contacts and set up a new profile with a new attitude. I could have stayed out in Asia the rest of the year – I felt free and really able to remember the old me, not the doormat me who'd spent all her time trying to be someone else for someone else. I am aware that I sound over the top here, but I defy any girl not to have had her 'weak time' where she gave everything to a boy and a relationship that was deeply unsuitable and that sent her a little bit mad. We all have that one boy who's done that to us. In my case, I am so lucky it happened when I was young and still learning. Trust me, even at twenty-five years old I am still learning. One thing I know for sure: rejection is never easy no matter how old you are.

When I came back from travelling the plan was to go off to Marbella pretty much straight away on a girls' holiday – it would be a massive test as Tony was going to be there on a separate lads' thing. I really was in two minds about going at all as I knew it could set me right back. I felt stronger, but deep down I knew that I wasn't over him and seeing him again was a risk. We all think we know how we will react in these situations. We play it over in our heads, we have it all rehearsed, exactly what we'll say and when, the great one-liners that will come tripping out of our mouths. It never works out like that and often the thing we least expect is what actually happens. To be honest, that's the only way I can explain the massive bust up with Tony in the middle of a club in Marbella on my first night there.

We had all planned Marbella before Tony and I broke up, so in my mind, even though I went travelling to get over him, I knew I would see him again. I think that's what helped me kid myself that I was over him, or maybe let me carry on pretending that we were just on a break and we would pick up where we left off. In my mind everything that had happened just flashed before me as soon as I saw Tony in the club and he wasn't giving me the attention I thought I deserved. I kicked off massively and I am mortified it was so public.

I suppose if I am really honest I thought he would have missed me madly and fallen into my arms begging me to take him back. How deluded was I? I began the evening on top form by playing it cool – I kept my distance, and I felt good about how I looked. (Obviously I had dressed up for him.) I was playing a good game but it didn't last long. The booze didn't help, I'm sure. I was there with the girls and all I could think about was him. My self-esteem plummeted and things went downhill quickly. I went mad at him in front of everyone, made the biggest fool of myself and ruined his night. Poor guy, he was just there for a few drinks and a dance.

I was mortified when I saw him the next day, so ashamed of myself. To give Tony his due, he really didn't give me a hard time. Perhaps he was relieved in a way that it was finally all over. I still see him out and about now we are grown up and we say hi, in fact I recently saw him at Nanny Pat's funeral and we had a chat. It is all fine now but back then it was a wake-up call. It was time to finish my A levels and get a life.

6

Glitz and Glamour

I'm not sure if it was a surprise to teachers that I decided to stay on in the sixth form and do A levels in art, media and drama. I was talking to my mum the other day about this. She said I would have done so much better at everything around that time if I hadn't been distracted by wanting a boyfriend. I know deep down that I made choices based on emotions and relationships that I shouldn't have and that have affected me to this day, but that's the way it is, isn't it? When you are a teenager and in love, you truly think you know it all and no one else has ever been in love before. Nothing felt right and I didn't commit to anything because I was always worried about what boys might think. I could kick my young self, but back then, obviously, I thought I knew it all.

I finished my upper sixth year and passed my A levels – I got a B and two Cs. Some of my friends, like Sam, had already been working for two years by the time I passed my exams, and now was the time to think about the big wide world. I had a clear head now and I knew I needed to sort myself out – it was all about the future.

All this sounded good on paper, but the reality was that I was a bit lost. Once we had collected the A level envelopes, we didn't really have a lot to do, so when Mark Wright approached Billie and me about going to work for him, we jumped at it. The work would be local and, realistically, would still mean plenty of time for fun. So we started doing some promotion for Mark when he needed us, delivering leaflets and waitressing at do's when required. In all honesty, it didn't ever feel like work as it was so much fun. We could have a drink and it wasn't exactly brain surgery. We didn't have to put ourselves out that much, and we spent all night with our mates and were paid for it – the perfect job for any teenager, really.

One day Mark called and said: 'There's this football academy in Loughton and I need you to help me out there as we have the contract to put on some events. The first one is with Mike Tyson.' Mark told us that Tyson was in the UK for the first time in years and was doing a Q&A at this academy. The idea was that Mark would help them sell tables, manage the auction, sell the raffle tickets, etc. The guy running the academy wanted two girls to come and specifically sell raffle tickets, so we said sure thing. It sounded like a right laugh and easy money.

We poured ourselves into these skintight dresses – me wearing a purple boob tube dress, so fitted I could hardly breathe, borrowed from my friend Gemma. I felt super-sexy and so grown up. I really remember thinking I'd made it. The whole thing was so Essex, and I think it opened my eyes to another way of living – going to nice places and having nice things. That's the thing about living in Essex: even before *TOWIE* came on the scene, you were always only a shoulder brush away from someone famous or wealthy. It has always been a fascinating place in that sense. Anything felt possible, in a weird way.

So there we were, Billie and me: all dolled up, hair, make-up, looking immaculate and ready to mingle. We certainly weren't going to let something small like having a job to do get in the way of having fun and making the most of this glam venue. To be fair, it was doomed once we started knocking back the booze because we became incapable of doing that one job. We got so carried away that we sold both strips of the raffle tickets, meaning that no one could ever actually win! We were simply milling around and drinking and chatting when one of the guys working with Mark came to find us. He said that Mike Tyson was out the back in a roped-off area of the marquee and they needed two girls to go back and serve drinks to him and his entourage. Off we went to check it out.

When we got back there the first thing we saw was Mike Tyson – you couldn't miss him because he is huge. He was sitting there, and the music was blaring as we were ushered in. We got chatting and he was really friendly. We got him some drinks and we started dancing a bit as my favourite song was playing (plus I was probably a combination of quite nervous and showing off).

Billie, never one to miss a chance to wind me up, laughed and said: 'Have a little dance with Mike, go on, Ferne!' So we did. Mike got quite into it all and you could tell he liked female company – he kept saying how pretty we were and what a good time he was having. You know when you look back and you think: How weird was that? I often think that. I mean, dancing with Mike Tyson in a marquee in Loughton isn't exactly run-of-the-mill stuff, is it? It was such a completely random day, but Billie and me showed ourselves to be good for the clients – we were friendly, chatty and people liked having us around and would ask after us.

From then on we became regulars. You can just imagine it – these two young girls straight out of sixth form who didn't have a clue what was going on, pouring drinks and getting involved; we thought it was hilarious because we loved this job, we couldn't believe our luck. They gave us ridiculous jobs from Monday to Friday to pass the time during the week. I had my first car, a Toyota Aygo that looked like a little toaster. I would wake up late and go and pick up Billie, and we would rock up whenever we wanted to, probably about 11 a.m., and then an hour later it was lunchtime and we would sneak out for a Wimpy. It was hilarious but we were smart enough to realise we needed to create a job for ourselves in a place like that – there was so much going on and the company Mark was working for were trying everything.

One weekend there was a party on a manmade beach; there were themed nights, polo matches – you name it, they tried it, and it was bringing all sorts of glamour to Loughton. There was so much money knocking around and it was such an exciting time. The likes of Penny Lancaster and Rod Stewart were attending parties we were waitressing at. It was mega exciting for two young girls and we were happy to muck in and do what we needed to. At the World Cup event we served beer in Germany football shirts and shorts – we weren't precious. In fact, we decided we were invaluable and one day we painted one of the little back rooms pink and said we were making it our office.

Part of our job involved leafleting for the academy, so we used to have boxes of the things in the boots of our cars and drive around with them for days on end – I am not going to lie, not every leaflet left the boxes in my boot and made it through the intended letterboxes. Now and then we did wander up and down the high street putting them through the doors of local shops and businesses, just in case someone checked up on us, but pretty much lots of them ended up in the recycling. It was naughty but it was classic teenage behaviour and we were all playing at working back then. It is the only time you can, really, before you have responsibilities and bills to pay. The priority was having a laugh now that school had finished.

All of this was fun and sounds great, but I didn't really

know what I wanted to do with my life and I was getting itchy feet and didn't like being bored. I had always worked, in fact I'd had a job before all of my friends during my time as a Saturday girl at the salon. I had always earned my own money and liked doing an honest day's work for my wages. I found it so satisfying – I still do. I didn't care what I did – shop work, the hairdressing, waitressing, bar work – I was never that teenager who stayed in bed till midday. Both my parents have always worked hard and that's something they instilled in my sister and me. We have all always had a job, that's just the way it is.

I had liked acting and did actually audition for RADA and the Central School of Speech and Drama, but it never felt right and I just didn't fit in. All the other kids I came up against there were quite snooty, to be honest; they had all been to the National Youth Theatre and all that jazz. They all knew each other already and it wasn't for me. (I'm not sure they would have appreciated my straight talking.)

I filled in my UCAS form, but I only applied to university for the sake of it, really. I didn't have a burning desire to go, it was just expected that you at least try. I think a lot of my friends went through the motions without ever really expecting to go. I applied with the intention of doing drama, but it didn't come to anything and I'm quite glad of that, especially given the path I'm on now. I've never really been good at rules and constraints, I'm much better doing my own thing and following my instinct. Plus I've never really loved the academic side – it was more the social side of school that I enjoyed. But despite that, around this time I did genuinely try to think about the future.

The girls in my group all went down very different routes, but the thing about growing up in Essex is that a lot of girls were looking for fame. This is a complicated one, as I know there's a certain perception of me – that I was so fame-hungry when I was on *TOWIE* that I was prepared to throw anyone under the bus, that I didn't care about anyone's feelings and I did whatever I could for storylines (none of which is true). There is also a certain school of thought that I spent years desperately trying to get on to the show and be part of what my mates Billie and Sam had. This is one of the many reasons I'm so grateful to have this book, because I can finally speak for myself. The truthful answer to this is multilayered. When you grow up in Essex it's hard not to get your head turned. I was lucky: I grew up in a nice house with nice things and it wasn't that I wanted fame to drag my family out of poverty or miraculously change my life – very far from it. The truth is that Essex allows the people who live there to have ambition and aspirations and I was no different from any of the many young local girls who wanted more. After all, that's why people apply to *Britain's Got Talent* or *The X Factor*: they want everything that goes with 'fame'.

In my case, yes, I liked waitressing at those glamorous events and I liked seeing others from Essex do well. Did I want to be a part of it like everyone else? Yes, I did. That was particularly brought home to me when Sam went on to start her career and was the first to become 'famous'. As a group we often used to say to each other: 'Surely one of us has to get famous?' And we did, just at different stages and times, but that didn't mean we were jealous of each other and couldn't celebrate our individual successes as they happened. There were some who signed up to glamour model agencies; in fact, a few of the original *TOWIE* girls started out like that and have continued to do it, and good on them. I have a lot of time for anyone who works hard and makes a living in any way they want to – each to their own. Most people like a bit of glitz and glam and if you don't, then Essex is not the place for you.

So yes, I wanted some excitement – what eighteen-year-old doesn't? With that in mind, it was great when Mark Wright asked Sam, Billie and me to come and work on some of his club nights at Embassy nightclub. We all had jobs, though I had the worst one: I took people's data – i.e. I was the annoying person asking for email addresses on the door so the club could spam them with special offers and 'news'. Sam would run the door and Billie would take people to their seats. We were all in the thick of it and having an amazing time.

Looking back, I do wonder how the hell we got by. I didn't have a proper job, just this Embassy work at the time, and yet we still went on holidays and had a wicked time out and about. Talk about clubbing on a budget! We would save up for Marbella, have spending money, plan our outfits and how much everything would cost down to the last penny. We didn't miss out on a thing and yet we didn't earn anything.

I suppose that Sam was the one who cracked it all first and had her head really screwed on – she had the job at the bank and also the Embassy one and she made the most of everything, she was so driven. It was a proper Essex bubble: Mark and Jack Tweed running these nights, Sam going out with Mark, Billie and me going along to help, and then a model agency came along one night and signed up Sam. It was like a different world back then and it is hard to explain, really. There were the likes of Lauren Pope and Danielle Lloyd flying the flag for the glamour modelling world – they were in the papers and in all the clubs and bars. Obviously Sam becoming part of that meant that we lived a tiny part of it too and it was exciting.

So Sam went on to enter a glamour competition called *Nuts* Babe 2009 and won. We were all behind her 100 per cent. I made badges so we could all show our support and she went around the country promoting; it was exciting to see it all taking off for her. Then came her pilot for *TOWIE* and that was it, she was making a name for herself. That's obviously her story and she has told it – but for me, I was proud to see my friend doing well and I suppose it did help me focus my mind. If I wanted my life to take off, I had to do something about it.

Evidence that I've always loved my food.

Matching PJ's and an early start on Sophie's birthday (Note the present for me too – Mum knew if she didn't give me one too, I'd have the hump!).

Above: Me, Mum and Sophie at Christmas – in our matching best again.

Left: Always shy behind my big sister.

Right: My first b[...] production and feeli[...] the nerve[...]

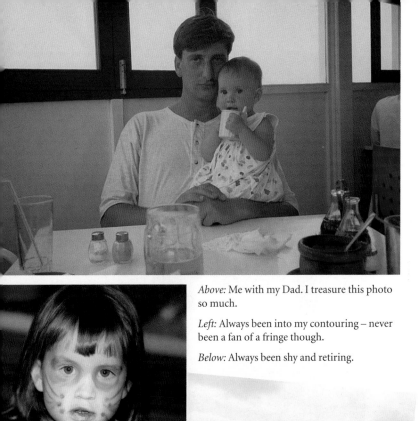

Above: Me with my Dad. I treasure this photo so much.

Left: Always been into my contouring – never been a fan of a fringe though.

Below: Always been shy and retiring.

Definition of awkwa
teenage years!

Below: Me and my
fellow prankster,
Billie, mucking abo
at school.

Me, Sam and Billie: the three Musketeers.

Awkward Teenage Years Mark 2: Bowling with my mum and sister.

Aged 17 and my first girls'
holiday.

Below: Aged 19 and always
a poser.

Sweet 16 and Year 11 Prom night with Billie – what the hell was that dress?!

Loving Life.

Loving Life.

This was my 24th birthday and Charlie took me to Chiltern Firehouse.
It was such a lovely night.

7

Charlie and the Fame Factory

I was still working at Embassy and I remember telling the girls that I wanted to try to focus myself. The truth is that I wanted a piece of what they had. That was all fine in theory, but in reality my mum made me sign on and look for proper work. It seems weird to say this, but I now realise that I have never actually been for a job interview. Everything I have done has been personality-driven. If I was interviewed I would be likely to say something like: 'Have me in your office and I will get the job done and make you laugh,' but who wants to hear that?

I ended up getting a temp job at All Saints that became permanent. It wasn't my dream career – at that time I didn't really have a direction – but whatever I did I made sure I did it properly. My attitude was always: however long it lasts, I will do it to the best of my ability (apart from delivering leaflets!). So I was a shop girl by day and a club girl by night, and then one day I woke up and thought: I will do hair.

I don't know why – I always said when I had my Saturday job that I never wanted anything to do with hair as a career, but it just hit me that it was the thing to do. This was doubly ironic given my hatred for my French plaits and having my hair cut when I was younger. Maybe it felt safe because of my salon training. Whatever it was, it felt right. I knew I'd missed the boat on the apprenticeship and I also knew I couldn't afford to take three years to get on the salon floor. So my dad kindly paid for a very expensive and intensive course at Vidal Sassoon. I totally threw myself into it and decided I was going to go the whole way and become a colour technician. I knew I had to work hard as my dad had invested in me so heavily. It wasn't long before I fell into the daily routine of travelling to London and back, colouring people's hair and living the salon life again. It was around this time that I met Charlie.

You have probably worked out by now that I have never been the shy and retiring type in any area of my life, and that applies to blokes too. If I like the look of a bloke I will just go over and say hi, I never worry about making the first move. What's the point in overthinking it? If you like each other, you will end up together anyway and it won't make any difference who made the first move. I think my mum summed it up brilliantly when she wrote me my letter in the jungle; she said that she was delighted everyone would finally get to see the real me: 'It makes me so happy people will get to see just how shy and retiring you are.' I love that my mum has such a wicked sense of humour.

I would always be the one to start off any situation and meeting Charlie was no exception. I met him catching the train going into London for my salon training. Every day for weeks I would get on the train, arrive at the salon and say to the girls: 'There is this absolute hottie who gets on my train every day. He wears an amazing trench coat – I think he's a Mitchells boy.' Now, a Mitchells boy is shorthand for a young, fit and beautiful boy who works in a branch of the high-end barber chain Mitchells. They have branches in Hornchurch, Brentwood and Chelmsford, and it's where Essex boys go for their big-time pampering.

Charlie made an immediate impression – I just loved

his look and his mole was unforgettable. I spotted him that first morning and he stayed in my mind. A few weeks later Billie and me were doing a bit of random work on the promotions side for Mark again and we were sent to an Essex polo match to do some data capture. As per usual we were having a great time, not least as part of the job involved going up to boys we fancied to try to 'capture their data' – it was hilarious – and then I spotted Charlie. He was standing talking to the ex-boyfriend of his sister Chloe. In true style, I marched right over and said: 'Hello. Can I take your number? It's for Funky Mojoe.' No intro, no explanation, just *bang!* – a question fired off.

I had a few drinks and carried on chatting, telling him that I saw him at the train station every day I went to work. Straight in there, I asked his age. He looked cute but he did look quite young – and I am just nosy anyway, so I wanted to know. He started to spin me some line about how he was the same age as me and I wasn't buying it, so I asked him what school he had gone to and he answered Brentwood County High, so that was the green light to bombard him with questions – who he knew, who his close mates were – and then give him a list of names I was sure he wouldn't know. When I was certain I turned and said: 'You're lying.' It turned out he was two years younger but, by then, it was irrelevant – I was quite interested. I didn't know what it was but I really liked his vibe.

I didn't see him for a while and then bumped into him one night out at the Slug and Lettuce – I do believe a lot in fate and how it puts you in the way of the people you are supposed to be with. He was there with his crowd and I was there with Billie and Sam. I decided he was too young when I spotted him across the bar. But as the night wore on I couldn't stop sneaking a look over at him, and I decided to go for it as we were leaving. We had just gone out on to the pavement to wait for a cab when I saw him coming round the corner in his car. I ran out into the middle of the road, slammed my hands on the bonnet of his car and shouted, 'Stop!' He looked terrified as I informed him: 'You're going to take us home. Now!' And that was it, we all piled in his car as I shouted: 'I've met you loads of times. Charlie, isn't it? Come on then, take me home!'

And he did – like a real gent he dropped everyone home and then he came into mine with his mate for a cuppa and we were having a real laugh, there was immediate banter and it all felt so easy right from the start.

As he said goodbye I remember we cuddled and didn't let go for ages. His mate Connor laughed and told us to get a room.

I always say that things with Charlie were easy. There was never any great drama (that only came after we joined the show), but the downside of no drama was that there was never any great, fiery passion either. I don't mean that how it sounds, as if we didn't fancy each other, because we did. It was just straightforward, and that's one of the things I loved most about Charlie and about being with him.

We started messaging on Facebook (everyone had moved on from MySpace by then) and went for a drink for a first date. It was a low-key drink in a pub, but we hadn't even sat down when he told me he wasn't wearing any pants! He explained that all the Mitchells boys told him not to wear any on the first date – I'm not sure what he thought that would get him, but it wasn't any more than a peck on the cheek and the promise of hanging out some more.

So that's what we did: we started spending time together and suddenly we were together all the time. I look back now and I can see how special it was. That first, young relationship is a beautiful thing because it is full of 'firsts'.

Obviously we weren't virgins, but being in a couple was new for both of us and I remember it being such a happy time as we had great experiences together – first holidays, first meeting the parents, Sunday roasts, sleeping over – it was the first proper relationship for both of us. I will be honest, I wasn't head over heels to begin with, but we were inseparable as time went on. We adored each other and had three and a half very normal and happy years until we joined *TOWIE*. We were so domesticated – I had changed a lot from the party animal I'd once been.

All the clubbing antics were long gone. Once Charlie and me got together I would be the first to leave a night out to be tucked up in bed early with him. I genuinely loved going home and knowing he would be there, and he didn't really like going out much. We were a very loving and affectionate couple and had our own ways as every couple does. I look back now and see that we must have seemed really soppy to others – we would call each other puppy panda and speak to each other in silly animal voices. (Once on *TOWIE* there was a scene in a shopping centre where Charlie had arranged for a big group of people to come dressed as pandas as a romantic surprise when we had got back together after a break.

I still remember how shocked I was at the effort he'd gone to.) They were such great times.

His family was very tight-knit and quite old school – his dad is a professional boxing trainer and his sister Chloe is obviously on the show. When I first met her I remember being bowled over by this head-turner of a girl with bright peroxide-blonde hair. She was a stunner. I didn't meet her for ages after Charlie and me first started going out; when we did meet it was at a boxing match at York Hall. She arrived really late in this massive fur coat and sat down with everyone looking. She turned to me and her first words were, 'Oh my God, you are beautiful.'

Given how things ended up between us on the show, it might surprise some people to know that once we were so close and genuine fans of each other. At the time we first met she was working for Playboy in Paris and when she heard I'd never been, she kept saying: 'You should come with me. I'll look after you and show you round.' She was so friendly and I was totally in awe of her. She was the most glamorous girl I'd ever met and had such a presence that it was impossible to ignore her. I mentioned that my mate Sam was on *TOWIE* series 1 – when I got together with Charlie the show was just airing and they were looking to add new characters to series 2, which is when Billie joined. Chloe had been asked (of course she had – I'll bet they were desperate for someone that glam), but she said at that point she wasn't keen. Isn't it funny how things can change so much that you don't recognise someone?

Charlie and I kept to ourselves mostly and didn't do a lot as Charlie didn't really like the whole party scene. (Ironic given what happened later when he joined the show and went to Spain on a boys' holiday.) But I remember one time that he said we had to go and support his cousin Joey, who was having an event at Revolution. So off we went. It was way out of our comfort zone – we were normally all about a Chinese takeaway in front of the TV – and yet here we were at this party with everyone from the show being photographed. I had brought Sam along – she and Joey famously hit it off, she made him get papped and the next thing you know Joey and Chloe are in series 2 of the show – and the rest is history as far as Joey and Sam are concerned.

TOWIE exploding on the scene was like nothing else, and it was the start of an era of TV that many have tried to copy. It was 100 per cent genuine and no one had any idea of the impact it would make and that it would still be going in 2016. Before I even start to talk about the show, the ins and outs and my experience, I want to make one thing clear: without that show, the producers and the fans, I wouldn't be where I am today. I may have decided to leave, but I will be forever grateful for what the show has given me – both personally and professionally. It will always hold such a special place in my heart. That said, we all know that I didn't have the smoothest ride and I will talk a bit about that later. (Don't worry, I won't go into every row I ever had or you would never get to the end of this book!)

Back in 2010 it was a breath of fresh air – suddenly Essex was on the map for everyone to see and little old Brentwood became an overnight hot spot. The show made Essex look full of buzzing clubs, bantering boys, dodgy cars, too much cash and lots of white teeth. The idea was that this cast would live out their real lives for the viewers to see and you would get to know and love the cast members. There have been a lot of books that detail the ins and outs of the show – how it is made, the arguments, the tears, etc. Obviously I have my own situations to tell later, but I'm going to try not to go over old ground about the show. I have no regrets or moans. That said, I am aware that I was enthusiastic and pretty much willing to do whatever they wanted for the sake of entertainment. I was up for anything and ended up being my own worst enemy.

When the show started I wasn't in the best place and, I won't lie, it was hard to see Sam and Billie being part of something shiny and new that was taking off when my life felt well and truly stuck. Yes, I was so happy with Charlie and I loved being settled in our relationship but, professionally, I wasn't where I wanted to be. I was working long hours on the salon floor, commuting every day and earning less than £1,000 a month colouring people's hair. As their lives took off and became a whirlwind of parties and press days and having their hair done and wearing amazing dresses, I felt as if I was wallowing in the boredom of my situation. I wanted something that felt so out of reach it would never be mine. I was happy for my friends, but I wanted it too.

Series 1 of the show was a smash and launched some of the most memorable favourites, including Amy Childs and Mark Wright. It was quickly followed by series 2 and Billie decided she wanted a piece of the action, so she joined too. It was then that things obviously started to change a bit for our group. Sam and Billie were tied up with filming a lot, the days could be long and it was hard to make plans as they never really knew where they were going to be and if they would be needed. In the early days the cast were also advised to spend a lot of time with each other as this helped storylines develop. It was all new territory and looked very exciting from the outside looking in.

People often ask me if Charlie's family liked me. Truth be told, probably not, as we were very different, but I have a huge amount of respect for them and I hope they saw that me and Charlie were happy for most of the time we were together. I adored that boy and we had a very special thing, he was the centre of my life and, when it ended, my whole world fell apart. Don't get me wrong, his immediate family were always welcoming (just as well, given I was at their house all the time), I just didn't ever feel 100 per cent comfortable. I'm not sure why really.

Charlie's and my relationship was very innocent in many ways, and we would never disrespect our parents' houses – we would hang out in each other's bedrooms and just chill. It was a lovely time – you could call it the calm before the storm.

8

TOWIE Time

I suppose you could say that, subconsciously, I always knew the show was the way I wanted to go. By the time I finally got there, I had already tried twice before, so it was definitely a case of third time lucky.

The research team in *TOWIE* are so incredible – they know everyone in Essex and do the rounds, making sure they talk with all the right people. It is about them finding anyone who can bring that extra something to the screen. It goes without saying that it's mostly drama they are after. The researchers are out and about all the time: they go to clubs, the polo, speak to all the friends and family of existing cast members, and follow on Facebook people who put photos up of themselves with the 'Essex look'. They are all over it – cast chemistry is vital to the success of the show and the right mix can bring incredible results. The people really do make or break the series, and the larger-than-life characters are never forgotten.

As far as my life had been going, I suppose I did it a bit in reverse. As soon as I got with Charlie I settled down to total domestic bliss. We were such a couple. Don't get me wrong, I still had my girls' nights out and my holidays away, but I always genuinely wanted to get home and see Charlie. I loved our life together. You might say that the disruption caused by my parents divorcing meant that I looked for security at a young age when others wanted to be free and single. It could be as deep as that, or it could simply be that I really liked spending time with Charlie – I did always say that he was my best friend and that was truly how it felt.

We had cute little routines during the week. We would go to work together and go to the gym together; he would pick me up from the salon every night and we would go home together – a proper middle-aged couple. If I look back at it, memories of those times make me so happy and cause me to smile. He was a junior training at Tullett Prebon, a global brokerage firm, with lots of prospects, I had my job at Sassoon, and we were a cool little couple.

He would call me on the salon phone to arrange what time to meet me or to check if I needed anything on his way over. I would tell him what time I was getting to Liverpool Street station and meet him at the pub over the road for a drink before we got back on the train to Brentwood. We stayed with each other every single night and were so close. We didn't earn much, but we always looked good and still managed to make our wages stretch to nights out at Hakkasan and days at the polo. I remember once, even though I had no money, I bought him a matching Hermès tie and handkerchief in a beautiful shade of red. He looked the business and so handsome.

Was he my first real love? Absolutely. Did I think we would be together for ever at the time? Yes, 100 per cent. But I suppose it was more of a friendship really, if I am honest. He made me feel safe and secure and I loved him for that. We were a team and he was such a lovely boyfriend – every girl should have a first boyfriend like Charlie to make them feel loved. But I can see now that it would never have been enough; your first real love rarely is, I guess. We had just fallen into being together without any great 'romantic chemistry moment', and, in all honesty, a certain element of passion was missing, especially given how young we were. I think that's part of why I like to do the chasing now with blokes: it is some kind of attempt to make sure there is passion and fire there right from the start. Although people think I can be a bit over-powering, when it came to Charlie and me, he definitely wore the trousers and we did things his way. I used to leave parties early to be with him and I didn't want to be out if he wasn't.

It was lovely and normal and probably a bit dull, living like a proper grown-up couple, but there is no doubt that our families and friends all thought we would get married. Despite me wanting to try to get on the show, Charlie tried hard to avoid the *TOWIE* circus. By then his sister and cousin were both on it, and my best friends were there too, so some social situations were unavoidable, like Sam and Joey's engagement and Chloe's thirtieth birthday party. On both occasions I remember us going, reluctantly, and Charlie just cringing and hating every second of it. It was bad enough when we were there getting papped, but then he would go into the office in the morning and the blokes would properly banter him about it and the fact that his sister was on TV, living out her life for everyone to see. The boys would watch every little detail so that they could do a wind-up number on Charlie the next day. It was all done in good spirits, but Charlie didn't like it much, I knew that.

I was still going out with the girls and I suppose they were what you would call 'famous' by then. Wherever we went the photographers were out in force and the pictures would end up in the *Daily Mail* the next day or in the *Mail Online* sidebar of shame. It was a whole new world, unlike anything I had ever been around. It isn't like now where I can take it or leave it, and sometimes it is plain annoying the way they follow you around and scream your name to get a reaction. Back then I loved seeing myself in the paper (even though it wasn't me they actually wanted to photograph – I was the annoying 'friend' they would always try and crop out of the shot before they used it).

We all thoroughly played up to it and once, as we were walking along the street on the way to a club, someone pulled my dress up and the cameras started to flash like mad. There I was, my dress right up and my knickers on show, all over the papers the next day. Not the ideal way of getting myself into the papers but a taste of what was to come.

The producers first got in touch with me as the show went into its fourth series. I got ready for my interview and went up to '*TOWIE* Towers' in Marble Arch. It felt like such a big moment and a huge step on the ladder to getting into the cast. In reality it was the opposite, and I had no idea how few of these meetings actually ended up with you getting on the show. I didn't tell a soul I'd been called up and I made sure I prepared. I look back and realise I sold myself so hard – too hard, it turns out – and in the wrong way. It was the time in the show when the glamour stakes were high and they had the likes of Maria Fowler on. Essex was buzzing, people were opening shops and other businesses on the high street: it really felt as though anything was possible for the people living the dream.

I went into that interview with the producers believing they wanted me to act in a certain way, that they wanted me to 'tell it like it is', so I gave them both barrels and started to slag everyone off. I was so harsh, totally playing up to the idea of a straight-talking, no-nonsense girl who would come on to the show to make waves; I was determined to show I wasn't afraid of making enemies. The producers were laughing a lot throughout the interview, but I never heard back – I wasn't surprised in many ways, after that performance. I'd misjudged it. I'd thought they wanted extrovert and gobby, and they did, but they wanted more too and I didn't give it.

When they had first approached me, the production team had made it clear that they wanted Charlie too, and that was never going to happen in a million years – he had been very upfront about that. We obviously weren't going to split up either, so there I was, back to square one. Although it felt as if all of our close circle were on the show, I stopped watching. I can't work out whether it was too painful to keep being reminded of what I wanted but couldn't make happen, or if I just thought that what I didn't know wouldn't hurt me. Either way, I tried not to have *TOWIE* on the TV.

I did sometimes go along for some of the filming. I would be telling the girls how exciting it was, and they would be saying: 'No, it's not, Ferne. It's such long hours and you never know what is going on.' It looked pretty good to me, so when the producers came back to me in series 7, via Sam, I went to meet them again. To be completely honest, I had previously asked the girls to put in a good word for me, and they had, but the people in charge were unpredictable. When it came to who they wanted, obviously it all depended on the dynamic of who was already on the show and whether that chemistry would work. At the start of every series they'd tap up loads of people, all sorts of different characters, really, and having already had one interview, I knew not to get my hopes up second time around.

This was around the time that lots of people who lived locally (and spent time hanging around the filming hot spots) were going around Brentwood saying: 'I got asked to do that show.' I used to think to myself: No you didn't – you just had a conversation that didn't go any-where like the rest of us, love. There were constant rumours that people were going on the show, that people were leaving – it was as if Brentwood had become its own mini universe, where everyone was obsessed with who was opening a shop, who was being paid what for PAs, who was trying to get their friends and family on the show. It was hard not be consumed by it, especially when you weren't involved.

Part of the sussing-out process for the show is to be interviewed and also filmed. When that happens it's hard not to think that you've cracked it and you are on, but that really isn't the case and it's all just preliminary. You are one of hundreds of people being seen, and so far down in the process of becoming a star on the show. So, armed with this knowledge, I went back a second time and did a scene with Sam on a handheld camera in her living room, and then I was filmed doing a scene on my own. It took a lot of time, and although I didn't want to get my hopes up, I was quietly confident. Again I didn't hear anything and I realised that I had to accept that it wasn't going to happen.

I was twenty-two at this point and thought: Get a grip, Ferne, and find another path. But it's hard when you really want something and you just can't seem to make it happen for yourself. The irony is that, out of all of us, I know it was me that everyone had expected to find the fame, as I was so loud and outgoing – but I am also a grafter who doesn't believe in giving up. Money was tight but I still got by – I suppose I just put my head down and got on with it. What I do know is that I never begrudged Sam and Billie any of what they had, far from it. We carried on going out (me on a budget) and I suppose I lived through them a bit. It was fun even if it wasn't my fun, if that makes sense. It was amazing that this experience was happening within our friendship group.

My final *TOWIE* meeting taught me that timing is everything and things happen when the universe is ready. So I was cracking on with life, things were good with Charlie and I was still close with the girls when Sam and Joey got engaged. As I said earlier, she has told her own story about their relationship and I certainly don't want to start wading in here, but everyone knows how up and down she and Joey were – it was all over the show for everyone to see – so I think we were all surprised to see them get engaged.

It was at their *TOWIE* engagement party that events finally took a turn for me regarding the show. I obviously didn't understand how the show worked back then, so was fascinated to be part of it. Joey and Sam were kept away from all their family and friends for the purposes of filming and had to make a grand entrance for the sake of the scene. So there we all were, their genuine friends mixed in with the *TOWIE* extras, waiting for the scene to be shot in a certain way; it was all very random. Being there as a real part of Sam's life but in a scene felt awkward, and I remember not really knowing how to play it – though I did genuinely tear up when they came in and everyone cheered. (The reason I'm going into such detail here is because this was the night I got 'spotted'.)

We all got drunk at the engagement party and I decided to get up on stage and sing. Anyone who knows me will testify that after a few drinks I am up for anything and love a good sing-song – I am never shy and this was no exception. There I was, surrounded by mates, as well as people I didn't know, and a bunch of producers for the show I desperately wanted to get on. So of course I decided the best thing I could do was to get on the stage and do an a cappella version of Paolo Nutini's 'Last Request'. (It would seem that Paolo is there for all the life-changing moments in my life – first my virginity, now this!)

So up I got on the stage and Sam and Joey started slow-dancing to my song. It must have been a car crash. (I have no idea where Charlie was at this point. Probably hiding away somewhere, pretending it wasn't happening.) I was singing my heart out when up came Gemma Collins: she began to sing 'Big Spender' and I was quickly booted off the stage. (That was my first experience of the GC and not much has changed.) After I had finished, I went to the bar and one of the execs came over. I thought this was my big moment, I really thought he was about to tell me how amazing I'd been. Over he came, turned to me and said: 'You sounded horrendous up there!' My big moment shot down in flames.

Anyway, life went back to the normal routine and Charlie and I celebrated our third anniversary in May 2013. I managed to lose my phone and, for some reason, didn't bother replacing it for about three weeks. It was unlike me, but I actually really enjoyed people not being able to get in contact with me unless they called the salon phone or I called them. I did check my Facebook messages every day when I got in from work and, one evening, I went into my inbox to find a message from a *TOWIE* researcher asking if I wanted to meet. Now this person clearly didn't have a clue about my interview history and the fact that I'd already been seen twice and turned down. For some reason it made me very angry and I just thought: No. Forget it.

I felt that they had messed me around twice already and had got my hopes up only for it to come to nothing. I had told myself that it wasn't going to happen for me and I was getting on with my life. I didn't want to be dicked around again, so I simply ignored the message. A few weeks later Billie told me the producers had come to her for help in trying to get hold of me because they couldn't get any answer on the number they had on file. She told them about my phone and so they tracked down the salon number and rang me there one night when I was clearing up. They told me they really wanted to meet Charlie and me with a view to bringing us on as a couple – the first time they would have done that. It was the exec who had heard me sing who'd asked the researcher to make the call!

It was weird for me: I had struggled so much with not getting anywhere the last few times that I'd started to tell myself that I didn't like the show anyway and I didn't want anything to do with it. Now here they were chasing me. Also, I knew there was no way Charlie would consider it, so while it was exciting and obviously I eventually did take the meeting, I still thought it was highly unlikely to come to anything.

There is no better way to get what you want in life than by being 100 per cent yourself. That's what I learned that day. I went in there and was completely honest, and it worked. I've carried that lesson with me ever since and remind myself of it all the time, even on *This Morning* and in any other job I've had. It is the key to doing things well and once you have the confidence to be yourself, you can do anything. Authenticity is the way forward, and I like to think that's why I worked so well in the jungle too – you can't live like that and put on an act, it's impossible.

But that day in the *TOWIE* interview I really felt I had nothing to lose, so rather than telling them what I thought they wanted to hear, I told them straight: I was very much in love with Charlie, he hated the show and didn't watch it, we weren't breaking up, so it was unlikely that I would be on their show if they only wanted us together. I then gave them my general thoughts on Sam and Joey's relationship, his ridiculous behaviour and the fact that at that time, I thought he was an idiot. I got it all off my chest, then I went home and told Charlie. I can't even begin to tell you how surprised I was when he told me that he would consider being on the show! He had changed his mind – the broking market was all over the place and he worried every day that he would lose his job, but I genuinely don't know what made him rethink it so completely.

What I do know is that, without Charlie saying yes, I never would have got on that show and I wouldn't be where I am today. Suddenly the timing was right and it felt as if this could finally be my moment. I was in love with my boyfriend of three years, finally I was getting on the show I'd wanted to be on for so long and I would get to film with my best mates. What could possibly go wrong?

9

Save It for the Scene

B y most standards, joining a TV show in its ninth series might seem late to the party, but that couldn't have been further from the case with *TOWIE*. Without a doubt, series 9 was the show at its peak and it wasn't going anywhere.

The cast was strong and full of people the public couldn't get enough of – Mario Falcone, Lucy Mecklenburgh, Joey Essex, Sam and Billie – but, more importantly, there were love triangles and dramas galore. With that in mind, bringing on a couple who had been happy and settled for three years and whose relationship lacked any of that high-energy drama was a bit of a risk for the producers (though I think they could tell we were going to be far from boring and quiet). They'd never had a long-term couple on the show and I know there were some cast members who thought it was the maddest thing ever.

On paper it made total sense: Charlie and Joey were family and Sam and me were close; Joey and Sam were at the centre of all the storylines with their on–off relationship and the viewers wanted more, and I would tell anyone who would listen that in my opinion as Sam's friend, Joey was the problem – so far, so good for the sake of explosive TV. What made the scenario even better for the *TOWIE* producers was that I had absolutely *no* self-edit button, so Charlie and I complemented each other perfectly. I would be honest and call it how I saw it, and Charlie was quieter, more considered and calmer.

I have had to think a lot about my motivation whilst writing this book. I know many people out there thought I would do whatever it took to get the biggest storylines or the most headlines, that once I got on to the show the fame went to my head, and I can understand why they might see it that way. The truth is much less interesting and calculating, however: I went on to the show truly believing I didn't have anything to lose and I was also determined to shake it up. It is very hard when you watch some of your best friends on a reality show because life almost becomes hyper-real. Here are people you know inside out and suddenly they are on the TV in your living room – it made the reality feel unreal and that became my biggest problem. I soon realised it was all too real, as were the consequences for me. Those cast members who'd started out in series 1 and were still there now had various business ventures and interests to protect. To my mind that meant they could be different on and off screen. In a way, if you get opportunities because of the show you become your own brand and I understand that needs protecting. It means trying not to get caught up in awkward arguments or show politics and not attracting any bad headlines. One of the reasons the show brings on so many new people at the start of every series is that the newer you are, the less you have to worry, because you haven't got anything to lose yet.

Did I want people to notice I'd joined and talk about me? Yes, absolutely – there would be no point in going on otherwise! I watched the show before I started filming and I knew immediately how I could play it. My mischievousness came out and I thought: Let's get it going here! Was it because I was fame-hungry? Not particularly, but I did see a massive opportunity to shake it up and reintroduce some straight talking into what had become quite a careful and considered show with everyone on their guard.

The one thing I instantly struggled with was the concept of 'sifting' – otherwise known as saving it for the scene. The idea was to keep things fresh by not talking about certain issues before filming, so that first reactions were genuine. It also meant keeping the focus just on the scene in hand and not going off track by bringing in discussions that hadn't been filmed. You can see it in my first episode. There was no doubt I'd arrived, but my naïvety meant that I had no idea of the unwritten rules. There were two that I disobeyed from the off:

1. Never bring an off-camera conversation into the scene.
2. Never slag off a much-loved cast member in your first scene.

Unfortunately I did both in my very first episode.

My *TOWIE* career started in Marbella when I was flown out for the special. After my meeting with the producers and Charlie's change of heart, I could tell they really wanted us – they proved that when they fast-tracked us through the whole pre-show process. It was a whirlwind. They interviewed me, then they taped me again and those tapes were sent straight upstairs. They came back immediately to say that they really wanted me and Charlie and that I couldn't tell a soul, so I didn't. I often repeat that old saying 'Loose lips sink ships', and I really do believe it. I'm also quite obedient when it comes to professional matters, so if they wanted me to keep it quiet, I would keep quiet. (Though I did tell my mum and sister, obviously.)

I had come so far I was scared of jeopardising it for anything. I was on an adrenalin high and my mum was so excited for me. She knew how long I'd wanted this and how happy it was making me – that was good enough for her. I'm sure that deep down she had some fears – I've never been the most diplomatic person and she knew what a straight talker I was but I am also not ever nasty, simply my own worst enemy. That is all fine within the family, but national TV is another thing altogether and I think she must have worried for me a bit. My sister also was cautious – she was anxious that I might put my foot in it and that things could get tough. As it turned out, I don't think anyone could have imagined the impact some of my comments would have in the end – least of all me.

TOWIE insisted that all new cast members get managers. It is so that someone has your back to guide you through and it's a very good idea as everything can be so overwhelming; Charlie and I decided to share one. So the next stage was to tell work. In an ideal world I didn't want to leave the security of my job – it was such early days and I had no idea if it would pay off. For all I knew, I would do one scene, be hated, and that would be the end of that. I had to think very carefully and not risk all I had worked for, but on the other hand I also had to give it a go – feel the fear and do it anyway. Work didn't ask me to leave, but they weren't happy about it and didn't make it easy. It was the beginning of balancing the tightrope of real life and *TOWIE*.

I was still at the salon and had this wonderful manager, Jerry. She was amazing to me but right from the word go, joining the show caused massive problems. Charlie didn't have any issue with his work: his boss was great and gave him the time off to fly to Spain for filming, no trouble at all, telling him he could just come back to work when he was ready. In fact, I think his work were more excited than he was in the end – no one could quite believe that quiet Charlie had changed his mind and was now going to be willingly filmed for a reality TV show.

My work were less enthusiastic. A head of department was less than impressed that I would be going off for two days but couldn't tell her why (as I was sworn to secrecy), when I had a book full of clients coming in for colouring. Plus I had to fly on a Saturday, which was the salon's busiest time. I asked for the time off and I was told no, so in the end we compromised and I took two days' unpaid leave.

I went for a coffee with Jerry to tell her I needed time off but couldn't really say why (though I sort of did!) She told me to go for it – though, hilariously, in the next breath she informed me that she would have to give me a verbal warning and discipline me for unscheduled absence. But she was so supportive and told me I would be mad not to do it. My head of department was so angry that she made me call all my clients myself and rebook them for when I came back. So with all that sorted, I packed and was ready to get cracking.

I do think it raised a lot of eyebrows, Charlie and me coming on to the show as a double act. People get the single characters because there is much more scope for drama, but two loved-up folk in a solid relationship not so much. A lot of the cast didn't get it, but Billie was chuffed – they told her for me, as they knew we were close. She was so happy for me, she knew how much it meant, and we couldn't wait to film together.

I flew out five days before Charlie to film the Marbs special that would launch series 9. It's funny what you recall from the big moments in your life. I remember at the airport my phone rang and it was one of my dearest friends. She said to me: 'This is all you've ever wanted, isn't it?' I'm not sure why that hurt so much. Maybe because it was true, in a way; I thought that I had hidden it well but maybe I seemed more nakedly ambitious than I actually was. We are made to feel that wanting something really badly is a negative thing, that ambition isn't attractive and that to want something others have is envy. I didn't ever envy or begrudge my friends their luck, I was chuffed for them, but I was so happy when I got a chance to experience it for myself. I don't think that's a bad thing and the world is big enough for everyone to do well.

At the airport I think the enormity of what was happening actually hit me. It was as though my whole body was moving through Southend airport but I wasn't really 'there'. My mum had dropped me off and as I stood on my own in the queue I thought: This is it. It's really happening. I suddenly felt terrified, but also weirdly confident that it would be okay.

The one thing I was determined wouldn't happen is that I be a one-series wonder. There have been a collection of characters who've come and gone, who lasted one series and then were never seen again. It became a running joke – James Argent was always the funniest about it – when we would do the cast photo shoots at the start of each new series. There would be a roll call as we lined up with hair and make-up done, wearing amazing outfits. The photographer would go through the cast list as he arranged us for the shot and Arg would pipe up: 'Where's Peri Sinclair? Peri? . . . Anyone seen the twins? . . . Where has Nanny Brighton got to?' We would piss ourselves laughing at the list of the disappeared ones. I was petrified that would be my fate.

I think if I had even entertained the idea of it not working out, then Marbella would have been a disaster. Anyway, I boarded the plane and I was so nervous it felt like the longest flight ever. I was seated next to a couple and I did my make-up just in case I was papped at the other end (very different from how I usually travelled, looking a right mess). I had arranged to go out with Billie and Sam that night, so was getting excited and also had no idea what to expect. The show was huge at the time and so, when I got chatting to this couple, I told them where I was going and that I would be in the show and they asked for a selfie with me – my first request.

I got to Marbella and settled in. The producers gave me a few days to chill out before I was filmed, which was nice of them as I'd expected to hit the ground running. I had two days of hanging around the pool while everyone else filmed and I wondered when I would get my first scene and who I would have it with – I really wanted to get it out of the way. In the end my first on-screen moment was at night, in a club – Tibu, in Puerto Banus. It was with Chloe, Sam and Billie, and I was introduced as Sam's friend. They didn't use a lot of that first scene in the end, and the chat that was included ended up being classic *TOWIE* banter and nonsense; I think Joey came out with the deep-and-meaningful line that if I was an animal I would be a tiger.

I got totally carried away with it all, as you might imagine. I was there in Spain, finally on this show and running around with Billie: it was a recipe for disaster. We finished filming and went out drinking, and the next thing I knew we were pulled back for a scene. The thing you have to remember is that I was all over the place; I've got booze, adrenalin and stress all swirling round my system and now I am tipsy, the last thing I expected was to be recalled for a scene. Suddenly, all I have waited for is here and I panicked I was going to sabotage it, at least, that's how it felt in my brain.

From the very start I didn't understand how the show could be a true reflection of people's lives if we only talked about half the things that happened. I thought a way forward was to try and encourage people to talk about situations that had taken place off screen. It didn't win me any friends, why would it when I had just waltzed in changing the rules and inadvertently calling them out. But I genuinely believed it was the only way to do the job properly. I know I arrived like a bulldozer, but I simply thought I was doing the job I was paid for; what was the point of me if I wasn't authentic? What I didn't think through was the fact that I was the one who would get judged because the viewers couldn't see what I could, so I just looked like a bitch.

I got involved and answered questions straight about the likes of Joey. (Producers: 'What do you think of Joey?' Me: 'I don't like the way he is playing Sam.') The scene that really got me into trouble on the first Marbs outing was when I accused him of crying crocodile tears. People didn't understand why I was saying what I was – all they were seeing on screen was lovely Joey, but I was bringing his personal behaviour to the table and it wasn't popular.

Don't get me wrong, in my head I didn't want to be average or boring. But did I cause trouble deliberately? No. What I did was provoke situations because I genuinely believed it made good TV. Did I know what I was doing? Yes. I thought I did but the thing with a show like this is the one thing that you can never bank on is someone else's response. I was only ever honest and direct so what really felt unfair was to be seen as two-faced. Anything I said was straight and direct. But when things are said and a week passes, those wounds are opened again and you are back to square one.

But I never do things with a motive or a plan and it doesn't come from a bad place. I never set out to intentionally upset someone. In fact, as far as I saw it in my first Marbella scene, my only wish had been to protect my mate, Sam, from the fact that she was getting the blame for her boyfriend's behaviour. People genuinely thought that all their problems were her fault, and it just wasn't the case so that made me angry. It all came to a head in one scene where Joey had cried on Chloe, telling her that Sam was a drunk and a cheat. I didn't believe those tears were real, and I said so.

We were all in Marbella to have fun, but the producers knew what they were doing in keeping us separated: it would only enhance the drama. We would all go out and party, and although Joey was staying in a different villa and doing his own thing, he still wanted Sam all to himself. At the time I felt it wasn't normal behaviour so I called him out on it, and as I've said, even Billie was shocked when they filmed me saying he was an idiot. I didn't tell anyone I had said it, so no one knew until the show aired and that's when it all kicked off. That's the other thing I hadn't factored in: it was all very well saying what you thought in the heat of the moment, but once things had settled down, the show then aired and everyone saw what you'd said, often out of context. The comments lingered, even if the row had moved on. All I felt I was guilty of was defending my friend.

My God, it caused so much trouble between me and the Sims family – Joey and Charlie's side were so angry with me. It was like my first strike and I'd taken all the pins down in one go. And Joey wasn't the only one I'd been vocal about out there. I also waded in on the whole Lucy Mecklenburgh and Mario situation. That's the other thing – I was the new girl and the fan base was loyal. There were characters who'd been there from the start and suddenly I arrived with an opinion on all these old-school favourites. It didn't go down well.

The problem I had with the whole Mario and Lucy thing was that seemingly Lucy got with other people while she was on the show whilst claiming she was in love with Mario, and yet he was seen as the love rat for cheating on his 'perfect' girlfriend. As far as I was concerned, it was plain to see that they were both as bad as each other. And everyone on the show did see it – they just wouldn't say anything. We'd all then get together for filming and everyone would pretend that she hadn't done anything and that everything was all Mario's fault. I personally found this bonkers, we were on a reality show and people weren't being direct. I wasn't stirring for no reason, it just wasn't the truth so I said it straight. It soon became a pattern: I would do a scene with a person, then do another scene and talk about that person, it would be aired and I would look like a snake. I had instantly painted myself into a corner I couldn't get myself out of; personally for me, the damage had been done before I had even got started.

Anyway, back in Marbs, Lucy sat on the end of the bed when we were in the villa with Sam and Billie and said:

'I went back with Dan last night.' We all speculated what had happened with Dan, and though she never gave details about what actually took place, I always felt it was unfair she chucked red wine in Mario's face and accused him of cheating on her. That is the thing about me, I never like unfairness in situations like that. At this point I have to say me and Lucy are still friends and I learned a lot after those early raw days, but at the time, I didn't realise the consequences.

To my mind the facts were there and my thoughts were simple: You've gone back to a very good-looking guy's place (Dan) after your boyfriend (Mario) has cheated on you in front of the nation. No one is going to cast stones. But don't play the victim. You've gone away, got carried away in the sun – that's fine, but at the time I felt like she should have owned her behaviour. But a good few years have passed since I came into the public eye and I have had stones cast and comments made – the one thing I have learned is that unless you are there, you never really know what has gone on unless you see it first hand. The other thing with the show was that they were always try-ing to keep up with the pace of our lives. Ultimately this meant that scenes had to be cut when there was so much going on – this meant sometimes my comments were seen without any context. Sometimes this would make me sound bitchier and that's why I always got a bigger reaction from the viewers. I get that's the nature of the show and have never blamed the show, but over time it did wear me down and get the better of me.

Charlie eventually came out to Marbs and filmed a scene that didn't make the cut. I did my stuff and no one saw what I had said until the show aired, by which time we were back in the UK. The Joey backlash was epic – both from the fans and from his family, but the Lucy backlash wasn't as bad. She did tweet the following and that was fair enough:

Finished my @lucys_boutique photoshoot now catching up on #TOWIM ... Wow she's soo 2 faced!! #b**ch

I am immensely proud of what Lucy has gone on to achieve and the way she eventually moved on and dealt with the Mario situation. She's a hard-working girl who has moved on with her life. Good for her.

I'd reverted to doing what I did in the first audition, which was not being myself but being what I thought they wanted me to be. I did pay the price and it was a sharp and pretty violent learning curve.

There was a moment later back in the UK when Rachel from Lime Pictures, the production company, sat me down with my press pack. This is the meeting where they go through all the headlines you've generated that week and help you through negative reactions. She used it as an opportunity to ask me what I thought of the rest of the cast. Now, it sounds as if I had it in for Lucy – I didn't – but I had said in an interview she was boring, so I said so.

I will never forget Rachel looking at me and saying: 'Are you sure you want to say this on the show?' But I knew I'd already said worse things, so my attitude was if you've done it, just own it. I wised up pretty quickly after the first episode, when I realised they had left in the Joey and Lucy stuff. I got wind of what they were doing later on when they were filming Joey and that hover stuff in the sea. We were on the beach filming a small bit on our own and the cameramen kept coming over and saying: 'We really want to show that he is a big kid.' They were saying things like 'Give us a look', and I wouldn't give it to them because I knew how it would appear. Let's face it, as far as Joey was concerned, I'd already done enough damage.

The Joey stuff caused real aggravation and had a big impact on my relationship with Charlie. For him it was the end of the world and he really made me feel bad for the trouble I'd caused. Back then, before all their own fallings-out, the Sims family were super close: no one disrespected the family, ever. When we first came back from Marbs (and after he had called me two-faced), I tried to clear the air with Joey by sending him a text message, but he refused to accept my apology. To be honest, I only sent the text because Charlie told me to, because he didn't want any problems between me and his family. Charlie was all that mattered to me and I would have done anything to protect that, but it all went bad quite quickly.

When the new series started, I watched the first episode on my own in my bedroom and I just thought: Shit. So, it seems, did the viewers. They thought: What is this girl all about? I tweeted:

That's right guys I tell it how it is! Like it or lump it I'm a #straighttalker

But as I sat in my room and watched the show, this wasn't remotely how I felt. I worried about what I had done and how it would seem to Charlie and Joey. But I also knew I had said it and there was no taking it back because the whole nation had seen it. Suddenly it felt indefensible and if I had tried to retract it then I would have been hypocritical.

Later in the series we filmed a scene outside with me, Joey, Charlie and Chloe – but Joey refused to make peace. Joey and I started to argue and Chloe butted in and threatened me: 'I wouldn't throw your weight around. Don't talk to him like that in front of me.' I stormed off and Chloe started to cry again, saying: 'I can't keep watching people being mean to my family all the time.' It was the beginning of the unravelling of everything, but I suppose I didn't have a chance to think of the long-term consequences of what was happening. I had arrived on the show with a bang and had to deal with the aftershocks.

10

It's Always the Quiet Ones

Charlie and me joining the show was like a bomb had gone off – I had arrived and people weren't fond of me from the get-go. Charlie had his thoughts and opinions too but knew much more about how to communicate them without alienating people.

My first series was bumpy, and I know it was my need to stick my oar in that perhaps made it harder than it needed to be. Early on I think I saw myself as almost like the viewers' voice – I tried to ask the questions I would want answering if I had been watching at home. Taking on Joey seemed reckless – he was erratic, and paranoid, but it was so hard for Sam as he was smashing it at the time and she was a bit in his shadow. When I kicked off about Joey, I meant it – I was on Sam's side because people didn't see the whole story – I certainly wasn't doing it to cause aggravation and get headlines. I genuinely felt for my friend and wanted people to see the truth. But I had no real understanding of the impact it would have on Charlie and me.

Joining *TOWIE* gave me a purpose and here I was, in a show where I thought people needed me to be extra entertaining and therefore I went over the top. But I don't think even I had any idea of the opinions people would have about me, mostly on social media. After that first episode the tweets came flying in, mostly negative but some people were supportive, saying I was a breath of fresh air and good on me for telling it like it is.

But it marked a line in the sand for Charlie's and my relationship. When we had got over Marbella, he apologised for me to his family, took me to one side and told me that it couldn't happen again. So was born his often-repeated phrase: 'Why do you do it, Ferne?' Interestingly, this was another difference between me and Charlie: I looked at the show as my job and, having started in this straightforward way, I now didn't feel I could cheat the viewers out of my honest opinion. Even much further down the line when I got into a row with someone about his relationship with his girlfriend and the way he treated her, Charlie would say to me: 'Why? Why is it you who has to point it out?' As far as he was concerned, I was giving too much over to the show and that was true. He also felt that my onscreen character was at odds with the Ferne he knew and how I had been for the three years of our relationship. I suppose things started to change immediately, really, if I think back with honesty.

I would promise Charlie I would tone things down and then we would start filming and I would speak my mind and so the cycle would begin again. It wasn't deliberate, it was that I thought these situations demanded honesty, or else what was the point? After Marbella it wasn't just Charlie I had to win back, I had to start again with some of the cast too, because obviously the whole Joey thing would have to be addressed on the show. After Marbs my next scene was back in Essex; I was being filmed dealing with Charlie's family to address what I'd said. Charlie told me they were fuming, so of course the producers wanted it all captured for the show.

You have to remember that I was living a split life. On the one hand I was living the dream, but on the other

I was still commuting into London every day and working a twelve-hour day on the salon floor, colouring and cutting hair. On the day I knew the big filming moment was coming up, I had been at the salon all day, so I did my make-up on the train and got myself psyched up for the bashing I was going to get.

We were scheduled to film at Frankie and Joey Essex's dad's house. I can still remember the nervous terror of not knowing who I'd be filming the scene with and how much of a hard time I would get. This was my first experience of the filming fear; it was so bad that I worked myself up into a total frenzy. That's the thing about the show, you never know who will walk into a scene or who will say what, there is no script so anything goes. When things have been tricky, you go into filming completely on edge. In my mind I could have been going to face Chloe, Joey, Charlie, even Frankie and Joey's dad. I travelled back to Essex imagining the very worst scenarios. By the time I got to Frankie's, I burst into tears with the producers – I think the enormity of knowing everyone had seen me saying those things and that I had hurt people really, really hit me. I knew it wasn't great and I was terrified that I'd caused long-term damage to people who meant a lot to me in real life. The producers were great and reassured me outside the house that I wasn't going into a pack of wolves. It was Chloe and Frankie and we had to do this, but it would be fine.

I think to any of the doubters, if you ever think I enjoy rowing and confrontation, just take a look at that scene – I am completely tongue-tied and chewing my nails. Look at the state of me! Actually, beneath the loud and opinionated Ferne is a young girl learning a new craft, with an amazing ability to put her foot in it, but I'm not nasty and I'm not a bitch. In the early days I would get so lost for words and overwhelmed it was embarrassing.

Both Chloe and Frankie could see that I was suffering big time – I had to do the bit where Frankie opened the door to me at least six times. I knew it must have been bad because Frankie looked at me and said: 'It's okay, really, we are all good. Let's just get through this scene and then we can chat.'

So I went in and Charlie was there, and they said: 'We just want you not to get involved in the situation. There are two sides to every story, we know that you are close to Sam and Billie, but stay out of it.' That was all fair enough, but the truth is that it was hard from the start since I was so anti-Joey, and Charlie was so anti-Sam. It was bound to cause friction between us but I don't think even the

TOWIE producers thought that Charlie and I would end up getting our own storyline off the back of it.

So I got through my first series, series 9, pretty much intact but coming across as being irritating and raising eyebrows – it felt as if every time I spoke it was to slate someone. Early on I created this role and I don't have the show to blame, but there were occasions later where they did use it to their advantage. I left myself open to it, really, but I was too busy to properly notice. Part of my eventual decision to leave was a need to distance myself from this pantomime character I had become on screen, but that wasn't really me.

At the time I didn't have a manager and it was a whirlwind of getting papped and followed as well as being offered all these magazine deals – a lot of it I wasn't even getting paid for, though at that time I was naïve enough to do stuff for free as I couldn't believe they wanted me. I'm a people-pleaser too, and part of me was just grateful that people wanted to talk to me. From the word go, though, I was totally for the show. Anytime I had a wobble, the producers would take me aside and say: 'You are brilliant – keep doing what you're doing.'

Most people played the game and tried not to get under anyone's skin. I spent a lot of the early days beating myself up all the time, but I know now that if I hadn't been like that, I wouldn't have been looked at twice by the *I'm a Celebrity . . . Get Me Out of Here!* producers. As I said earlier, I have come to realise that being myself is fine and by far the best way.

But I was on a massive slippery slope: I was in the public eye, I knew I had to play up to it and I was losing myself to the circus of the show. I felt like I was starting to lose the real me, and it makes me really sad when I think about it now. I never started to believe my own hype, but one of the things that made it so hard for my family and for Charlie was what they saw as my split personality. In his eyes I was being portrayed as a monster on the show, and away from the cameras, I would go home and ask Charlie what we should do for dinner as though nothing had happened. It was so messed up, I can see that now, but I still saw it as a job. What I didn't understand is that the negativity seeps into everything and you can't undo what you've done on screen, especially when people see what you've said about them.

For a while that was how it went. My work self and my real self were completely separate, though both my 'selves' were loving life and we were gearing up for a trip to Ibiza. We had finished my first series, Joey and Sam had split up, Billie had met Greg and Charlie and I were adjusting to playing things out on camera. We had some time off after the end of that first series and before filming for our second series began, so we decided to do a girls' holiday to Ibiza. Sarah, Sophie, Sam and me rented a tiny one-bedroom apartment and had *the* best time. Even though he and Sam weren't together any more, Joey decided to have his birthday bash there too and Charlie was flying out for that.

I won't lie: I was surprised at Charlie going on a lads' holiday. He even hated clubbing locally in Essex on a night out. But I had noticed a real change in him after our first series. He'd hated socialising before, and now here he was flying over to Ibiza for Joey's do. He hadn't thrown himself into the whole '*TOWIE* experience' like some of the other boys, he hadn't got many PAs off the back of it all, he wasn't the club/late-night type and he wasn't really the sort to flirt. I felt 100 per cent secure, but maybe slightly intrigued at this 'new Charlie'.

My Charlie was just a normal boy and the relationship was nice and calm – no drama, but as I've said, no major fire, and I was maybe feeling that a bit more after we joined the show. In some ways Charlie wasn't always perfect for someone like me. He never wanted to come to family parties, and if he did then he always left early. I would be the first on the dance floor and Charlie would be in the corner, thinking about how quickly he could get home.

Anyway, I was happy that he was getting out and about – that he was getting out of Essex. I flew out first and he was planning to fly out a few days later with Mario and Tom Kilbey to make up the rest of Joey's gang. Off I went knowing that I would see him in a couple of days, though I knew I wouldn't get much time with him as he was on a boys' holiday and that meant limited contact with his girlfriend. I was totally cool with that, as I knew the rules.

Things were a bit tricky this holiday as Sam and Joey had split up and it affected where we could go and the mood of the holiday. Every girl knows that feeling after you have broken up – you can't stand to be near your ex but there is a part of you that still wants to know what's going on, and that is hard to avoid somewhere like Ibiza. It's such a small place and everyone knows where everyone is – it's a bit like Essex, really.

It was hot and fun and we got on with the holiday. On Sundays in Ibiza everyone goes to the Ocean Beach club, but Sam just didn't want to go and have to deal with Joey and all the drama, so we went somewhere else. Charlie landed really late, and looking back now I can see that right from the start he wasn't messaging me much.

In terms of where we were at this time, we had that first series under our belts, our faces were known but we weren't main characters with big storylines or anything. Back then I could never have predicted that I would go on to do another seven series, right the way up to series 15, as well as all the specials in Vegas, Spain and Tenerife. I was still at Sassoon part-time and it was the start of fame; we were still peripheral characters that the public were getting to know. We hadn't earned any loyalty yet and we weren't a big deal in comparison to some of the others. We were still completely loved up and, like any couple in the same place for a holiday, I'd thought it would be nice for us to meet up quickly for a little kiss and a chat, so I suggested it. After all, we were only over-lapping for two days.

Joey was seeing a girl who worked out there, we thought it might have been to make Sam jealous. The thing about Ibiza is that it can often become a big round of paparazzi set-ups and photo opportunities. We didn't want to be part of it so we stayed away from all the obvious places and did our own thing. We totally respected that Sam needed to be away from it all.

I texted Charlie and didn't hear back. I did think it was weird for him not to just send a little text, given that we used to text hundreds of times a day normally, but he was there with the boys so I was determined not to cramp his style. That night we were out, I drank too much and wanted to go home to the hotel, so I did. When I got back I plugged my phone in and got Wi-Fi. Suddenly all these tweets started to come through from people who were at Ocean Beach, telling me they'd seen Charlie snogging some girl. There were even a few tweets saying he'd cheated.

I started texting him, saying: 'Why are you not texting me back?' and he got properly angry (very unlike him), replying: 'For fuck's sake, Ferne, I'm here with the boys.' Then I just didn't hear back. Now, I have to reiterate here: he was a devoted boyfriend who kept in touch at all times, nothing was ever too much trouble for him, so this was mega weird behaviour and obviously I had an inkling all was not well. In fact it was more than an inkling; from the minute those tweets came through, I just knew deep down that he had cheated on me. That night spent waiting for him to call back was the longest night of my life, it was pure torture and I did not sleep a wink. The pain was real and physical, my stomach would not stop churning.

It was my first time in Ibiza so I didn't know the layout of the place or the names of the key places. I heard they were going to Plastik bar, which was in fact a small place and not on one of the multi level clubs. Anyway, we had this pap out there who was there to take set-up photos of people in the public eye. He was splitting his time between all of us and so knew everything about what we were all up to. I decided to ask him to do some investigating. I asked him if he had been to Ocean Beach, because I'd had these tweets telling me that Charlie had cheated. He said: 'Look, I'm not going to lie to you – there were these girls hanging around and it looked a bit shady.'

I hadn't heard from Charlie at all and I now know that in those missing hours he'd taken the girl back to his hotel and had sex with her. I finally heard from him that evening when he eventually returned one of my many calls. He sounded relaxed: 'All right, babe. You having a good time?'

I played it cool and decided to do some digging on Twitter. I found the accounts of some of the girls who were supposed to have been there, got their numbers and called them to find out what was going on. I could never do that now, but back then a) I didn't care! and b) no one really knew who I was. These girls were happy to tell exactly what was what.

Apparently there was a picture of Charlie with his arms around a girl. (It ended up on the front page of the *Daily Mail* a few days later.) The girl was wearing a gold sequined bikini and they had their arms wrapped round each other – it wasn't exactly a 'hello, how are you?' hug. The girls I spoke to on the phone didn't hold back and told me: 'It properly looked like you were separated: he didn't mention a girlfriend at all.'

It isn't okay to behave like that when you are in a relationship and for the newspapers to capture and flaunt on their front pages. Charlie had only slept with me and one other girl, so I could understand why he might have his head turned, but it was so out of character for him and I had a really bad feeling about this girl – she had that look, she wanted him, and those girls stop at nothing as fame is all they care about.

I finally got hold of him and begged him to meet me at Plastik. He said no, he needed to be with the lads, not meeting up with his girlfriend. We had never had this situation before: we were such a tight couple, we were practically married and never played games with each other. Charlie had never given me a single reason to feel insecure or doubt him before and would never have acted like this. I wasn't overreacting, I knew this was very bad news for us. I had that pit-of-the-stomach feeling. The girls couldn't believe it and just kept saying: 'Are you sure, Ferne? This is Charlie we're talking about.'

My head was utterly wrecked and my heart was shattered, I didn't have a clue what to do for the best. I was due to fly home the next day and had to be in work, but I couldn't even think about going. In all my adult life I have never pulled a sickie but this was an exceptional set of circumstances, I was desperate to speak to Charlie because this was our life, our relationship, it was my world. My flight was due to leave at lunchtime and my genius plan was to call in to the salon, say I had food poisoning and turn my phone off so that they couldn't hear my international dialling tone. The flaw in the plan was that I kept having to turn my phone on and off to check to see if Charlie had called. I felt desperate and lost. Why was he doing this to me?

Despite everything, he wouldn't answer his phone all day, so I decided to go to his hotel and confront him. I called ahead to find out if they would tell me his room number from reception – I thought that was the best way to catch him red-handed. The hotel wouldn't tell me a thing but I went over anyway and waited.

I eventually got hold of him and we met outside the hotel, though I wasn't allowed to go to his room. He sat me by the pool and we bumped into Lauren Pope, who looked concerned as I was sobbing at the table. I just felt so confused and scared about what I was about to find out. I was in such a state, Charlie didn't know what to do with me, and he just kept saying: 'What is wrong with you? Nothing happened.'

I demanded to see his phone so I could go through it. He was clever: he knew I would ask to see it so he'd got Joey to text him saying: 'Tell Ferne she's got nothing to worry about, blame me. Those girls were all me.' The boys were all back-covering, which was typical.

I eventually went up to his room as he got ready to go to Ocean Beach. He said he needed a shower. (Talk about priorities!) He could see I was desolate and he just wanted to get back on it. I didn't recognise this man in front of me. So we went up and he took a shower. Obviously while he was gone I went looking for his phone, but he had taken it in with him and hidden it under the sink while he was in the bathroom. It was such guilty behaviour and I lost it: we had a scuffle in the toilet and he kept telling me I was mad and paranoid.

I couldn't get any sense out of him. He was closed off and acting like a total stranger. Eventually there was nothing I could do as he ushered me out of the hotel and told me he would give me a lift so I could catch my plane. I ended up getting into the car with him and Mario, which meant we couldn't talk about it in any great detail. It was so surreal: I suspected my boyfriend had cheated on me, he was denying it and, instead of comforting me, he was driving me to catch my plane so he could go to the beach and carry on partying. To top it all off I was in the car with Mario, who proceeded to give me a long speech about how this is just what happens to happy couples on *TOWIE* – that Lucy had to put up with it all the time. He said that girls were always lying about sleeping with him (!) and trying to wind Lucy up, that sometimes he would be on a PA and she would actually be there and girls would still be tweeting her, saying that he was cheating.

Mario is a dear friend now, but back then I wouldn't have trusted him as far as I could throw him. And he was the expert at covering cheating tracks – he wasn't the one I wanted to be talking to, that was my boyfriend, who was too busy getting ready for another day at the beach. Despite the boys trying to style it out I knew deep down. I've always been one of those people who believes there has to be a grain of truth in rumours that blow up – you can't just pluck a rumour out of thin air. I knew what he had done, no matter how much he denied it.

I got back to the hotel and the pap was there. He said he'd heard from one of his mates that there were photos of Charlie kissing this girl doing the rounds and about to get printed. Just like that, *boom!* – the confirmation I'd dreaded. (Later down the line I found out it was actually that same pap who'd taken the shots, but there you go, that's the press for you.)

I was beside myself, calling Charlie again and crying, begging him to leave Ocean Beach (where I knew he was with those girls) and come to see me before I flew home. I mean, was it too much to ask that my partner of three years, who I believed to have cheated on me and who had been caught out, would want to come down and reassure me and actually talk to me before I flew out of the country? He just kept saying: 'It isn't true, I don't know what to say.'

I begged him: 'If you loved me you would come and talk it through. Don't leave me like this.'

I suppose he couldn't face me. Whatever the reasoning, his behaviour after the event was as devastating as the fact he had cheated on me. Now, with a lot of hindsight, I can be more rational about the whole situation (though at the time I was too distraught to think straight), and if I put myself in his shoes he must have thought all his dreams had come true. There was this young, pretty girl (I wouldn't have said that at the time) who was a lot of fun, throwing herself at him. (She didn't make him work very hard for her by sleeping with him the first night she met him.) He was one season into one of the biggest reality TV shows, he had lived a sheltered life, and now the boys had taken him under their wing, showing him the fun he could be having. Of course he'd had his head turned. To be fair, we had been together a long time and you get into a rut, don't you? This girl was exciting and he felt like one of the lads for the first time in his life. It was hard to compete with that. What I didn't expect was for him to show me no decency at all in the way he handled it.

The show had changed the one constant in my life and I don't think even Charlie knew what was happening to him or how out of character this was for him. I had to go home on the plane knowing that he'd cheated on me but didn't want to see me to work it out. I'd told him there were pictures and his response was that there couldn't be as he hadn't done anything, that it wasn't true and that the pap was lying.

I boarded the flight with Sam and had to keep my phone off because of work, so couldn't keep texting him. I sobbed all the way home, my head on Sam's lap as she stroked my hair for the whole flight. I'm sure she was hurting over Joey too and we were two girls on the way back from a holiday where two boys had disrespected us. She scooped me up and got me through that flight home and I will never forget how she put me first and looked after me. I was heartbroken, truly broken, and I didn't think it could get any worse. How wrong I was.

11

Lyin' Eyes

There is nothing to compare with walking in from the worst holiday ever and seeing your boyfriend kissing a random girl on the front page of the *Daily Mail*. At that time me and Charlie shared the same agent, which didn't work in either of our favours as she didn't really do anything to try to contain the story. I left that agent pretty quickly after all this hit the headlines. I can't tell you how that affected me – it was the worst thing I had ever been through. I got back from the airport and fell through my front door. I couldn't talk, think, cry even. My mum was there and I was devastated – I think I just hugged her without saying anything for ages (very unlike me). No one expected it from my Charlie and that was a big part of the shock I felt.

I couldn't eat or sleep or go to work for two weeks. I had never experienced pain like this, even the salon were easy on me because my life was suddenly splashed all over the papers and they knew exactly what was going on. The day after I got back, I called Charlie. (He hadn't called me once.) I left him five messages before he picked up the phone to me, and he was still out when we spoke – maybe even with her for all I knew.

When I did get hold of him I tried to keep it together. I asked him if he had seen the *Daily Mail*. That was the moment I found a glimmer of my old Charlie: now it was in the papers he was unable to deny it any more and he burst into tears and started sobbing down the phone. He kept saying over and over: 'I am so sorry. I'm just so sorry.'

He didn't know why he had done it and was terrified that it was all out there for everyone to see. To be honest, neither of us could believe it, we were in shock and didn't really say a lot. Before he had called me back I'd been on the phone to his mum, who was as much in shock as we were. I told him on the phone that if he really loved me he would be on the first plane back to try to work it out.

I didn't understand why he couldn't see that the worst thing about this whole scenario was him staying out in Ibiza to party. He stayed out there for another four days while I dealt with the fallout.

This heartbreak was different from anything else. With Charlie the feeling was of utter betrayal: now I truly knew the meaning of the word disappointment and Charlie had done that to me. I loved the bones of this boy: he made me feel so completely secure, he was my routine and I didn't know where to go without him. He was the one person I shared everything with, who I turned to for everything, good and bad. He was the only one who could make me feel like it would all be okay and yet he was the one breaking my heart. It was mortifying that everyone knew and I was full of disbelief. I wrote two sides of A4 outlining all the questions I wanted him to answer – when he did eventually go through the list, his answer to every single one was 'I don't know'. I genuinely believed him. I'm not sure he ever really understood himself why he did it – what hope did the rest of us have of working it out if even he didn't have the answers?

I spent two weeks in my mum's bed as I didn't want to be on my own, and things didn't even really change when he eventually came home – though while he was still out there in Spain his phone was always switched off and I would be reduced to calling Joey or Mario, who would make up an excuse every time I got through, saying that Charlie wasn't available. It was as if he wanted to cut me out completely and wait until he was home to deal with me. I wasn't sure whether to laugh or cry talking to Joey and Mario on the phone.

If I did manage to get Charlie to pick up, I would say: 'Do you not want to be with me?' But he would just say yes and change the subject. For me the only thing I could focus on was the fact that he was staying out there in Spain despite all the pain he'd caused me. Did that mean he was still sleeping with her? I would torture myself – perhaps his attitude was 'in for a penny, in for a pound'? After all, he had been caught now and there was nothing he could change to undo that. Maybe he thought he might as well make the most of me being in England and him being there with a girl clearly into him. I couldn't catch him twice after all, and the fallout couldn't be any worse. I drove myself mad imagining every scenario, and part of what was so hard wasn't just the cheating but his supreme lack of interest in coming home to comfort me and fix things.

I tried to go into work but just broke down so I was sent home. It sounds so dramatic and a bit mental, but I really thought I wanted to die, that life was over and I was worthless. I found out when he was due home (early the next morning) and so I clung on to the fact that we would finally get to talk it all through.

Except that I didn't hear from him. I sat at home waiting all day for him to be in touch. Nothing. I bombarded him with texts – my mum was telling me to leave it and that if he had so little respect for me there was no point trying to force him to behave properly, but I was *fuming* with him. It was utterly disrespectful and I had pinned so much on him coming home and finally explaining it all to me, then he just ignored me, after the humiliation of him being on the front pages.

It was too much and I finally lost it when he did eventually text to say: 'Do you want me to come round?'

I couldn't believe what I was hearing.

He came round without his phone, which immediately wound me up – why, if he had nothing to hide? Then came the lies and the tears: he swore he hadn't slept with the girl and that it had only been a kiss and a cuddle. He went on to tell me that he was so sorry for the whole thing but that all it had done was make him realise that he wanted me but that he was also massively confused.

I didn't know whether I wanted to punch him or hug him. It was like talking to a complete stranger. I was straight with him and tried to stay calm. I said: 'Do you want to be with me or not, Charlie? I need a simple answer.'

We were sitting in his car behind the church next to my house. I didn't think it was a good idea to actually have him inside the house with my mum (she was still so angry), and we couldn't go out anywhere because the story was all over social media. It was one of those real 'be careful what you wish for' moments – I was trapped in a living hell, reading about my life in the papers and online. I'd thought that when Charlie got home that somehow he would have all the answers and we would get through it. But there I was sitting in his car, faced with someone who was as lost as I was. Neither of us had the answers really, and I was so confused.

I had spent so long wanting *TOWIE* and all that went with it, I hadn't factored in the bad bits and the fact that when I got it, I seemed to lose all the good things in my life that mattered most to me. I knew that if I hadn't got us both on the show we wouldn't be sitting in this car park having this conversation, contemplating ending things. I wasn't in a good place. In truth I was so angry and I didn't care if he thought I was being mental. Here I was telling him we could get over it, that I would try to forgive him, and all he kept saying was that he didn't know what he wanted. This wasn't how things were supposed to go in my head. The final straw was when he said that this whole business and being away from me had made him think that maybe he needed some time to be single.

I got out of the car and ran off, through some trees behind the church. I think I might even have been screaming. I remember thinking how desperately I wanted him to come after me – I wanted some kind of show of love from him after all he'd done; I needed him to show me he wanted me and I needed him to know that without him I didn't care about living or dying. It was all very dramatic, but they were some of the deepest feelings of my life. I can't explain what it felt like to have the one person I trusted with my life not only betray me, but then not fight for me or what we had. That's the worst feeling in the world – looking at the other person not giving a damn and wondering if you were the only one to think it was special.

He caught up with me and we talked some more. He still didn't know what he wanted, but he agreed that we would go out for my birthday a few days later – he'd booked tickets to see *The Bodyguard* and we could take things slow. I couldn't really believe what I was hearing – how do you take things slow with someone you've dated for over three years and you think you know inside out? Having been the cheater he was now calling the shots, but I was too dazed to care really.

I wanted him on bended knee begging me for forgiveness, but I clearly wasn't going to get anywhere near that. He didn't even seem to want to fight for it. I always say that the irony is that people might have expected it from me but not from him. I decided to take back a small bit of control, and I'm sure every girl who's been heartbroken will identify with that. I wanted the other girl to think that we were just fine, even though we weren't. It was important that she didn't think she'd won. So I went to our joint manager and told her that I wanted her to arrange for Charlie and me to be papped coming out of *The Bodyguard*. It was my way of showing people that I was in charge, that it was my decision if I took him back, and I didn't need any snide social media crap calling me a mug. At that moment I wanted people to think we were back together and that girl meant nothing to either of us and at the time I didn't care if that made me look weak for taking back a cheater. Charlie had told me he wasn't talking to her, so this would be a nice little message to her that we were just fine, thanks very much.

It felt weird getting ready to go out on a date, for my birthday, with the boyfriend who had broken my heart, but I spent ages doing my hair and make-up and felt sick and excited all at once. That all changed when Charlie eventually turned up on my doorstep. If I'd been expecting any great romantic gesture I was very much mistaken. He stood there holding a card and a single red rose that he'd bought at the train station – this from a man who'd surprised me with a Cartier watch on my twenty-first birthday.

I put aside my hurt and threw myself into the situation. I began by tweeting that we were going to *The Bodyguard* – mainly so I could later explain to Charlie why the paps just happened to be there as we came out. It was easy enough. After what he'd done it was no wonder we were seen as front-page fodder, of course they were going to stalk us down.

At this point my friends weren't on board – in fact they

161

begged me not to go at all, as did the salon girls. It's hard to explain unless you've been there. It was all about putting myself back in control, even if it meant swallowing my pride. But deep down I was full of anxiety about the prospect of breaking up. I loved him so much but his actions – both the cheating and his reaction to it – had sent me into a self-confidence spiral. I became anxious about everything. We were going to Sushisamba for a pre-dinner drink and on the way I asked him if he would stay at mine that night. He said no because he was worried we would have sex. To my mind, that would only have worried him if he was still seeing that girl.

He had no idea how much I needed him to be with me that night but he said he didn't want to and I just couldn't understand why. The night descended into a bit of a slanging match. We got the train back home and I cried all the way. He just couldn't understand it. He kept saying: 'What are you crying about for Christ's sake, Ferne?' and getting angry with me. (I've always thought that is the sign of a guilty conscience.) I told him I was at my lowest ebb, that what had happened had killed something inside of me and I didn't trust myself to be alone. That seemed to sway things. He came back to mine – my mum was not happy, but she let me get on with it. That night he wouldn't even touch me. All I wanted was a cuddle, some show of remorse, but I got nothing.

Now I know there will be some of you out there thinking: What a mug, and I can see why you might think that – looking back I think it too. But at the time, in my mind, it was simple: I didn't want to break up with him, I wanted us to try to get through this. I thought that, given that he'd cheated on me, I would be calling the shots, but I hadn't considered the fact that, having cheated on me, Charlie might then be the one who wanted to walk away. It didn't make any sense in my brain and I was terrified I was losing control. At that point, I was prepared to do anything to hold on to him. I was so weak and sad – I hadn't eaten a thing for six days and all I wanted was his arms around me.

The next morning, while he slept, I took his phone from his trouser pocket and went off to my mum's bathroom, locking myself in and going through the whole thing on a mission. I saw a text from Tom Kilbey asking how it had gone with me and whether I was fuming. Charlie had answered: 'Not great mate, I need to speak to you.'

Everything else was deleted. I went through everything – Safari history, emails, social media, everything. If anyone ever wants a private investigator on their ex, I'm your girl!

There were two missed calls from a random number that he hadn't saved, so I decided to call it. If he'd been clever he would have filed it under a fake name and then it wouldn't have stood out to me so much. But I was on the case and, making the most of my chance, I scrolled and dialled. A girl answered with a giggly 'Hello'.

My heart dropped. I said: 'Hi, it's Ferne here. I'm sitting here with Charlie now, so do you want to tell me why the fuck you keep ringing his phone?'

She put someone else on the phone, who started some story about how they were trying to get hold of 'another Charlie' and that they couldn't talk right now as they had a family emergency. That was it – in came the anger.

I walked into my bedroom, shook him awake and shouted right in his face: 'You lying cheat!' I threw the phone at him and I went mad. He had lied and lied. Okay, he wasn't sure he wanted to be with me, okay, he wasn't as sorry as he should have been and maybe he was a dick for wanting to take it slow, but now he had lied to my face. He swore he hadn't heard from her and that it was over. I was screaming the house down – my mum came running up to see what was going on.

Charlie looked terrified. He was screaming my mum's name, telling her to get me away from him, saying I was mad. He got up and scrabbled around, putting on his suit and that amazing Hermès tie I'd bought him. That bloody tie! He didn't even have time to put his trousers on properly before he was running down the stairs shouting at me: 'I'm going. You're mental!'

I started to cry, begging him not to leave. I told him I would forgive him.

He left shouting at me as he legged it down the road: 'I don't want this. This has made me realise I do not want this.'

I didn't hear from him again until 13 August, when the *Daily Mail* ran more photos of him and the girl having lunch together in London – just five days after my birthday night out and the pap shots of us. So the night that I thought I was showing the world we were fine, this girl was waiting in the wings believing that he was going to dump me for her. The day the story broke I called him. Strangely he was the person I needed to speak to the most about the situation he had caused. It was so screwed up. I was at work and a total mess and having to put up with everyone talking about me on the commute into London, as it felt like every day there was a new story. It was such a hideous time – he didn't even call me to let me know the pictures were coming out.

I called and called and at last he came on the line. I was standing outside the salon, sobbing and telling him I just didn't understand what was going on and who he had become. I think in his head, after he'd left my house, we were done and he didn't have a girlfriend any more. He told me again that he didn't want us, and his way of driving home that message to me was to go out on another date with that girl and do his own pap set-up.

Enter the Find My iPhone app, the best and worst invention ever in the hands of a girl with a broken heart. This app ruled my life and allowed me to know where Charlie was at all times. Others let the *Mail Online* or Twitter rule them; for me it was this app. All you need to track the phone is your Hotmail account and your Apple ID password and I knew his so, *bam!* I could tell where he was *at all times*.

So that day I spoke to him, he told me he was going to play padel in Canary Wharf with his mates and that he had nothing else going on. I saw that his phone was going to Canary Wharf to play padel – that was fine, but then all of a sudden he was the other side of Canary Wharf in a hotel. I had seen on the other girl's Twitter that day her going on about how she was back from partying in Ibiza and she was looking forward to some healthy sushi later.

All of a sudden Charlie's iPhone was at Roka, a Japanese restaurant. That was it. I just lost it and told the girls at the salon I was going to confront him there.

I told my mum and she forbade me from doing it; even my dad rang to tell me not to. I genuinely think the situation was sending me mad; I will admit that during this time I didn't exactly make it easy for him to think about coming back to me. I was acting insanely. I didn't go in the end, which was just as well because his phone stayed there for ages and I'm assuming it doesn't take three hours to eat sushi, even if you can't use chopsticks.

One morning I was getting on the train at Brentwood to go to work and his phone said he was at the Premier Inn just up from the station. I couldn't work out what that could mean, until it dawned on me that she had come to Essex for the night but he obviously couldn't take her home to his mum after everything that had happened. (How very romantic that he put her up in the local hotel.) This was confirmed when I looked at her Twitter account later and she had posted that she'd driven to Essex.

I was behaving like a classic heartbroken girl, I suppose, feeling hurt but then doing the things guaranteed to make me hurt more. It was like picking a scab: the more I felt hurt at him not wanting to be with me, the more I looked, the sadder I got. I drew the line, though, at knowing he was bringing her back to be on my doorstep – he was taking her to Lot 75, which was a favourite for lunch and where my mum goes all the time. I think what hurt me most was that he was clearly into her. A silly little fling would have been one thing, but he was treating her like his girlfriend and I was gutted.

Or so I thought. A mere three weeks later he was papped stepping out with *Geordie Shore*'s Vicky Pattison, pictures yet again courtesy of the *Daily Mail*. (It felt as though they were the official photographer to my life.) They'd originally met in Ibiza (when he cheated on me) and they'd exchanged numbers then (though he didn't cheat on me with Vicky, just the other girl he got papped with).

Anyway, Charlie and Vicky followed each other on Twitter and shared lots of banter. I remember thinking: Where has my sweet, kind, caring, considerate boy gone? And when did he get replaced with someone who has banter with other girls on Twitter, right in my face, even though we weren't together any more? Looking back, I can see it was the early signs of someone who wanted to be free, though it was a disrespectful way to go about it. It had nothing to do with Vicky – she wasn't my boyfriend, *he* was. This was the boy who never left the house and was now behaving like a proper Essex lad.

Anyway, fast-forward to when we had split and I was still tracking him, and I noticed on the app that his iPhone was going through the Dartford Tunnel. Now, a few days earlier he had bantered Vicky online and she had said she had a PA in Kent. It couldn't be a coincidence that he was in the same area of Kent where her PA was. I then watched as his phone came back towards London and stopped at Sushisamba, so I knew what was happening. It still hurt when I saw the pictures in the paper, though – the final piece of confirmation that he was young, free and single.

Don't get me wrong, Vicky didn't owe me anything – I think what hurt a bit was in her book she said that when she met Charlie he had told her he wasn't happy with me. It was hard to read that in the book of the girl I suspected my ex had had a thing with not long after he dumped me. You could see from when we met later in the jungle that there were no hard feelings; there was no need to hold a grudge as she had nothing to do with my break up. Actually, when I met her in the jungle it was like a clean slate. I was able to take her at face value, nothing to do with Charlie, and get to know the girl that I have come to see as a close friend. It is funny how things turn out, we are so tight now and she is a loyal friend who I know will always have my back.

There were so many girls being associated with Charlie at the time and it did make me even more confused about the other girl, the one he cheated with, in a way. One part of me was happy that she was out of the picture (and judging by her Twitter feed, she was pretty fuming herself), but part of me was sad because it really then all just felt like destruction for nothing.

I had been put in a situation that was totally out of my control; I didn't want to be single but Charlie had forced that on me. My whole world had been turned upside down: I was coping with fame, my boyfriend had dumped me, my heartbreak had been splashed across the papers and I was about to leave my job. That summer ended up being one of the best and worst of my life. I often find that when I hit rock bottom the only way is to pick myself up, turn around and take another direction, so that's exactly what I did. I went to a party with some mates and met some east London boys, and decided to start seeing one of them to make myself feel better. I knew it was time for some changes and I felt strong enough to think about what they should be. My second series of *TOWIE* (series 10) was about to start filming and I had to try to build a new life that didn't involve someone who clearly didn't want to be with me.

12

Overlap

The first thing I had to deal with was my work situation. I think both sides knew it couldn't go on the way it had been, but neither party wanted to do anything about it. I'd been starting to feel increasingly bad for my manager and my clients at the salon because I knew I wasn't able to give my all when I was there. I really didn't like pulling the sick day and I knew what I had done was bad. With so much going on and already feeling my life was out of control, I knew I had to leave in the end. It was such a risk but I didn't want to get the sack which could easily have happened due to the fact I kept asking for time off. My head and my heart weren't in it and it wasn't fair on the salon or the customers, so I jumped; it was a

172

huge relief to leave on good terms and I still love popping back in to say hi to everyone.

Summer 2013 turned out to be both the best and the worst – I jacked in my career, I had split up with my boyfriend and the *TOWIE* fans seemed to hate me for saying some harsh thing about much-loved cast members. I was heartbroken, really, and struggling to understand what had happened to the Charlie I loved, how things had broken down so badly that he'd had to let me know he didn't want me by setting up pictures with other girls. It introduced me to a period of massive self-doubt about myself: the way I looked and everything I did. I wear my heart on my sleeve and there was no disguising the fact I was well and truly shattered.

If I'm honest, I've never been 100 per cent happy with myself and a lot of it is an act. I feel very strongly about this as I worry about girls coming up through their teens now – social media isn't going away and it can make us all feel so crap about how we look. I am the first to admit I'm guilty of wasting loads of time scrolling through my Instagram, looking at other girls and thinking about how pretty/thin/amazing they are. If you feel down or delicate at all, looking at people's 'perfect lives' just makes you feel more down on yourself. We all know deep down that any social media site is all smoke and mirrors – we only put the good stuff up there. It's self-editing taken to extremes, of course we want to show off our best selves to the world but on social media, it can feel extreme.

I suppose I have always thought of myself as a bit odd-looking. By that I mean I'm not classically good-looking like some girls. I know that when I get glammed up I can pull it together and it's all good, but I've never looked at myself and thought: Wow, you look beautiful! People think I'm confident about everything, including my body, but what I say is that you are given what you're given and you just have to crack on with it. I don't moan on about stuff; I'm never going to be a size 8 and I certainly won't starve myself trying.

I will always be grateful to my mum for giving me a strong sense of self-worth and the idea that I can do anything I put my mind to. I do think that has helped me cope with my physical hang-ups and it certainly helped me deal with bitchy comments – first in the playground and then on social media. I still get shocked at what people think is acceptable to say to you online when they've never even so much as met you, just because you're on their TV screen. I always say: Fine if you don't like me, each to their own, but there is never any excuse for getting personal on someone. That's another thing about *TOWIE*: I might speak my mind but I'm never mean or personal – I've only ever done that once and I was mortified (more on that later).

I suppose we all have our fair share of playground bully antics and I got off quite lightly in the grand scheme of things. There was one girl who was awful – it was one thing the boys calling me Goose, but when another girl did it I was appalled. We were in a maths lesson; she got thrown out and for some reason thought it was my fault. On her way out, loud enough that I could hear, she looked and me and said: 'You fucking goose.' I hated that so much and thought it really broke the girl code. But it's all about not showing they've got to you, isn't it? If you don't leave yourself open to others they can't get into your head.

People have always felt the need to comment on either my nose or my height. Tony and his group called me 'Longshanks' and though it was meant to be affectionate, it hurt because it was directed at my height – an area I have always been sensitive about. I've got very good over the years at brushing it off as banter, but often your big insecurity is the thing that gets picked up on and highlighted – we must give off a vibe or something. People have always had something to say, and thought they could get away with it because I covered it up well. Once I joined *TOWIE*, every imperfection I struggled with was fair game. Complete strangers think they have the right to an opinion and that they can comment on the size of your thighs, your nose etc. It's like open season on you, and you can't react to everything because there simply wouldn't be the time!

My nose has always been a problem for me and I've spent much of my life toying with the idea of a nose job; I just felt if it was less big somehow I would feel better about myself. I suppose if people spend long enough pointing something out then it becomes impossible not to make it an issue. The thing I loved (and still love) most about Charlie is that he used to tell me I was beautiful all the time and that he adored my nose. It was actually a beautiful thing, the way I would get upset about it and he would kiss my nose and tell me it was the best part of me.

But seeing myself on TV was devastating. I remember the first time I caught sight of myself on the screen I almost cried: all I could see was my nose. I got used to people feeling they could have a say on whether I was too fat or too thin, on what I wore, on my hair and my make-up. This was all done mostly online (the keyboard warriors always have plenty to say after an episode) but also out and about. I can't count the number of times I've been down the high street and been stopped by someone giving me the ultimate backhanded compliment (though I am sure it isn't meant like that): 'You look so much better in the flesh.'

As I've got older, though, I have become more annoyed by how unrealistic everything is now for girls. There is no innocence any more and life is so competitive. When did life goals all become about being skinny? I refuse to be drawn into the madness: I love my carbs, I'm healthy but I don't go to the gym as often as I should, I don't drink enough water. But you know what? I live my life and try to be happy. It is important to look good and feel healthy and I know I have to look good for my job. I do try to be moderate but I'm not going to lie, I love my cocktails with the girls, I love cheese, I love bread and I just want to live my life. I have to remind myself not to be bombarded or blinded by skinny models and bloggers who present the perfect front. I often wonder how happy they really are.

I suppose I wanted to address image and confidence here as, in the late summer of 2013, my opinion of myself was pretty low. Charlie had cheated, had been pictured with a string of gorgeous girls, and it had made me feel worthless. We had split but, a bit like with Tony, it was hard to consider it truly over as I knew I would be seeing him again very soon. We started filming series 10 (my second) in the September, just weeks after all the *Daily Mail* headlines, and I knew things would be awkward. But then we started to meet up before we began filming again, at Charlie's request, after he'd had some kind of realisation that he wanted to get back together. We met in a parked car (which seemed to be our way) and he poured his heart out.

We began meeting up again and going on secret dates, but I was too embarrassed to tell my friends – I didn't even tell Billie. It reminded me of a scene in *Sex and the City*: Carrie starts seeing Big again but doesn't tell the girls, then is caught early in the morning leaving his apartment by Miranda, who has a dentist's appointment in his area of town. You feel embarrassed at seeing that person who has caused the pain, and you know your friends will be pissed off since they got you through all the hard times, but you can't help yourself.

I hate to make it seem like I'm defined by boys, but any girl who's been cheated on will know that part of recovering your self-esteem involves taking back the control. He had messed up and now he wanted me back; it helped me heal and I started that next series feeling more and more myself again. I felt as though I had the upper hand and, as we prepared to film the Vegas special, I was in a good place.

But, as ever, the show made things hard for Charlie and me. We were fine in secret as long as it was just the two of us, but lines immediately got blurred once filming commenced. He had started coming back round and we were going on Nando's-and-cinema dates. He was trying hard, but we hadn't had 'the chat' about what we'd both been doing whilst we were on a break. Now, I hadn't really been doing much except seeing this guy from east London who was a bit of a rebound to help me try to get over Charlie. I had no idea what Charlie had been up to.

So off we went to Vegas, sort of back on but very much keeping it to ourselves. I did say to him one night that if he wanted to try to make it work he had to tell me everything; he gave me his version and we went off out to a film. I left my east London boy behind and had the best trip of my life – it was the biggest special they had ever done. The girls got really close and it was so glam – we had the most amazing suite, me, Billie, Lucy, Sam and eventually Jess, too, as she had split up with Ricky Rayment. We were living the dream – pool parties, filming etc. Charlie was there in the back of my mind and I hadn't told the girls. I think part of me was a bit worried that the show would take him down the whole 'love rat' path after the recent headlines, and if I was seen getting back with him, people would really think I'd lost the plot. After all, there is only so much sympathy you can have for a girl if she allows herself to be constantly mugged off.

One night I was talking to Charlie and we came up with a rather mental scheme that he should get with Jasmin to take the heat off us and use her as a decoy. She had shown an interest in him before and it would be the perfect cover for us to carry on and see if we could fix what was wrong. It also felt important to take care in how we presented it to the viewers too, as they had seen so much drama and Charlie hadn't been great. It was the first time we would be back on screen together. It sounds a bit weird but this was my life. I had loved this boy and he had broken my heart and now we were being thrown together again. Imagine having an ex you still love and having to face him for filming and being tangled in storylines the whole time.

In my mind, he could get with her and then realise it was me he wanted, meaning that we could get back together and come out in the open. It was daft, really, and we didn't need it, but I think I was just nervous about the reaction and whether I could trust him not to hurt me again. It wasn't helped by him randomly posting a naked selfie, which yet again made him look like a player. I felt as if he and his management were trying to turn him into another Mario, and just as I got closer to trusting him, something else happened that made me worry about his commitment and whether I could believe in him.

The selfie ended up opening a conversation about how many girls Charlie had slept with since we'd broken up. He said twenty-seven! (Me and my mum did the maths and worked out that was three girls a week from when we had split until Vegas.) But I still loved him and wanted to be with him – rejection does shadow everything and it makes you do weird things. I first found out about this during one big scene out in Vegas where I ended up bringing all my feelings into the scene (as I often did). I had been drinking and was with Billie getting ready for our next bit, and the exec came over to us to have a word. I couldn't work out what was going on and then she said one thing to me: 'Ask Charlie how many people he's slept with.'

I opened the scene by telling Charlie I had slept with East London Boy. I really thought he would be shocked that I'd slept with anyone at all, and in all honesty I suppose that, despite the fact we were trying to put things right, I was still really angry at what he'd done. Plus he had taken things too far with Jasmin and had actually snogged her, which hadn't been part of the plan.

So there I was, looking him in the eye and telling him honestly that I had slept with this boy and had been seeing him. He looked at me and said: 'Yeah? Well, I've slept with twenty-seven girls,' and just looked at me. I lost it; it felt like the ultimate betrayal. I could not believe it, twenty-seven girls?! Especially when I had been the second person he'd slept with and we had only been broken up for one month, thirty days! So I threw a drink over him. He always knew how to get to me and things were always full of drama, but the aggravation never lasted with us. I got into trouble with the producers for that incident but we put it behind us and carried on falling back together.

I look back now, though, and I think: Imagine having to hear things like that for the first time on screen. This was my actual life being used for a storyline. Gradually more people found out and he upped his game: he did the big panda shopping centre thing; he came round to Gemma's to make a big speech about how it was me he wanted to be with. The truth is that being back with him made me feel safe but I think we were both masking the damage his cheating had done. Perhaps we were naïve to think we could get our relationship back to where it had been, but we tried. So we slipped back into the old routine, things were good and settled again and the girls had accepted we were back together. All was calm until one night when my friend Sarah had a birthday dinner in December 2013 – enter Hurricane Frank Major and all the destruction that came with him.

Sarah, Sam, Billie, Sue (Billie and Sam's mum) and me went out to celebrate at Roka, Canary Wharf. We had a lovely dinner and then decided to go clubbing afterwards. Billie was pregnant so went home with Sue, but the rest of us headed off to Funky Buddha on a random Tuesday night. It wasn't even busy but we wanted a dance. In we piled and went to the bar to get the drinks in. We were getting quite drunk and as the club started to fill up, I bumped into this boy. Not the best-looking boy but so charismatic he made an immediate impact on me. In my usual style I got straight in there and said: 'I know you – I went out with a mate of yours!'

I have always been great with faces, I remember everyone, and it came to me straight away that he was Frank Major. He had to get me water as I was quite drunk, the girls had gone back to the table, and I can't explain it: something just clicked inside me. We instantly hit it off, me and this Essex boy meeting in London. I'd never really met him properly, just heard of him, and here we were.

There are times, I believe, that the universe steps in and that night was one of those moments: I was meant to bump into the man who was to be one of the biggest catalysts in my life, at just the time I needed it most. It was like a lit touch paper and it was so unexpected. He was, in many ways, the opposite of Charlie. Immediately I could see he was the life and soul and he made me feel good about myself. I went back with Frank Major that night – while I was meant to be getting things back on track with Charlie.

He lived in a house in Chelsea. He was just so much fun, wanted to talk to everyone, find out their story, find a way in with a conversation. He was curious and gregarious and so vibrant. Charlie preferred to go home and never got involved with my friends much; not that I minded, it was just that Frank was totally different. Even on that first night meeting Sam and Sarah, Frank was at the centre of the action at all times and I fell for that big time.

God knows what came over me, but I ended up going

back to his and staying the night. I left in the morning smitten, even though I was heading straight to see Charlie. I knew what I was doing was wrong, but it just felt right and I left his the next morning feeling happy and guilty all in one. Frank knew instinctively how to look after a girl; he got brownie points for organising a car to take me back to Essex – I ruined the classy gesture by getting the driver to pull over five minutes up the road so I could open the door and throw up!

I got into my house and I rang him straight away to tell him what had happened with the driver – even at that early stage all I wanted to do was hear his voice. I climbed into my bed to try to recover before starting work, and rang him again. We spoke for an hour, then I had to get ready for my clothing launch. It was then that it hit me: Charlie would be coming out with me to this do and I had just spent the night with Frank. It genuinely wasn't revenge on my part for what Charlie had done to me; I'd simply got swept away by Frank and I had this need to be with him. He invited me round to his the next night just to chill (and recover from my hangover) but I was too paranoid to go. I felt instantly guilty now that I'd had time to digest it and was terrified Charlie would find out. The last thing I wanted to do was hurt him.

I went round to Sam's for dinner and ended up talking about Frank all night and texting him. He invited me over and I just jumped in the car and drove to Chelsea because I needed to see him. We took a huge risk and went out. Again, looking back, I don't know why – anyone could have seen us and taken a photograph. We went to a bar that was absolutely packed – it was right before Christmas – and it was like being on an exciting early date. The chat was great. Frank is a really clever guy and he would teach me stuff; he reads loads and was interested in everything, not just the small, gossipy world of Essex.

I genuinely believe that you have to be so lucky to meet someone at the right time, and I do think he was the right guy at that right time for me. Things with Frank and me had the potential to be everything that an adult relationship should be, only the situation was complicated by my unfinished business with Charlie.

On the few occasions I went to Frank's it was really relaxing – watching films, chilling, drinking, finding out about each other. One afternoon while I was there Charlie called to tell me he had two tickets to *Anchorman 2*. I was mortified, and I remember looking at Frank and admitting: 'I have to go.'

Frank completely understood and was great about it. I was in a panic as I had nothing with me to change into and hadn't expected to be going anywhere. So Frank swooped in to save the day: not only did he arrange a car for me, but he sent his driver to Topshop to buy a dress and shoes and gave them to me to wear. There aren't many men who would arrange a car and clothes for the girl they're seeing to go and meet her boyfriend.

It sounds bad and it was: it was everything that I'd found so unacceptable in Charlie's behaviour and I suppose it was hypocritical. Turning up dressed in those clothes, having come from Frank's place, it was 100 per cent wrong. It definitely brought things to a head because I finished with Charlie within the week. I just couldn't do it to him. This was not the way I behaved and I wasn't about to make it worse. I still recalled very clearly how desperate I'd been when the roles had been reversed; I knew how bad it felt. He didn't deserve it any more than I had.

Finishing with Charlie was the hardest thing I'd ever done. I simply told him that things weren't right, despite how hard we had tried. I don't think either of us could believe it – just four months earlier I'd been hanging on to his ankles, begging him not to leave me, and here I was in his kitchen telling him that it was over. He obviously quizzed me massively to see if there was anyone else. I said no. I know that technically this was a lie, but the truth is that I didn't know what Frank was to me, let alone what Frank and I could mean. It was exciting and different but it was new and I had no idea where it could lead. There's nothing worse than a girl who goes on a few dates and then acts as if she's marrying the guy. I didn't want to rush into anything. I liked Frank, and that was enough to make me realise that I had to make things clear with Charlie so there were no blurred lines. I didn't dump Charlie for Frank – it was more that spending time with Frank showed me that I didn't want to be with Charlie any more. That was the moment I realised we had run our course. I was upset, but felt quite calm and okay – I was determined to do the grown-up thing and treat everyone properly.

I'd done a lot of soul-searching. I think that I knew before Charlie cheated on me that I wasn't 100 per cent happy, but what we'd had was special and comfortable and I hadn't wanted to rock the boat. Being cheated on changed me and changed us, so even when we'd got back together I think we'd probably both known it was doomed. Frank came in to show me that Charlie needed to be out. Charlie and I talked it through – he was shocked and I felt a bit numb from the conversation. Afterwards I went straight round to Billie's and burst into tears and then I felt weirdly calm. I knew I had nipped it in the bud and it could have been so much worse: it was one week of overlap.

Things carried on with Frank and me and I felt a lot happier with the truth being out in the open and knowing I was doing the right thing by everyone. Me and Frank saw each other over Christmas – it was lovely and we started to spend a lot of time together. That said I also tried to keep things low key: I was still raw from splitting up with Charlie and I knew he was hurting too, the last thing I wanted to do was disrespect him or rub it in. It was also important to keep things with Frank out of the public eye. Charlie had cheated on me and the whole world had read about it; my romantic life had been played out enough and I didn't want any more headlines about my love life. We didn't get papped together and no one ever knew about Frank Major until he put himself out there and surprised me by joining *TOWIE*.

He had an amazing pad but wanted to go out clubbing all the time. He made a huge effort with my mum, he called her Gilly, and he worked hard with my friends too (always a good sign in my book). He really pulled out all the stops when Sam had a party for her birthday just before New Year; he arrived all dressed up and armed with every single MAC make-up item that she loved in a box as a present. For Billie's birthday he went especially to Harrods to collect the Monica Vinader necklace I'd bought her, he was so thoughtful like that.

Me and Frank were together three months in total and it was intense wooing like nothing else. It helped put me back together again and give me back my confidence, but I wasn't ready to commit to a full-on relationship. I had genuinely started to enjoy being single and I think finishing with Charlie had given me the courage to stand on my own two feet again. It felt good to only have myself to answer to and I wasn't prepared to give that up. I was beyond confused.

But just as I'd felt as though I was gaining some control over my life, yet again the show threw it into chaos. I backed myself into another corner by letting my heart guide my head and I started seeing Charlie again. It was the classic problem of the show dictating my real life – filming brought us together again and we fell back into each other's lives. It's very difficult to make clear decisions about your emotional situations when you're filming because you don't get the breathing space you would in normal life. Filming and being in scenes with people after a fall out or break up is really difficult; in real life you would avoid them but when you're filming you're thrown together. We were best friends and splitting up left storylines hanging that being on screen together meant we had to deal with.

It was now January 2014. Sam had gone into *Celebrity Big Brother* and I was looking after her Twitter account; I stayed in every night as I was doing Dry January and I could spend the evenings watching the show and tweeting. But as I geared up for filming I knew I would be back in Charlie's life and the hectic madness would start up again.

Our first episode back involved some time away for Mario's birthday in a posh country house, and I was struggling – there's no other way to describe it, really. I wanted to be on my own, liked being around Frank (though the gloss was wearing off and I could see how little we actually had in common), and every time I saw Charlie all the old feelings came flooding back. I felt quite good because of Dry January, but I think, if I'm honest, even back then I was struggling with the constraints of *TOWIE* and what being on the show did to my life. It felt like I would film, it would be chaos, and then during the time off it would all settle down and I would find my rhythm, only to have it all fall away when we'd start the next series.

I don't want this to be a moan – after all, I know how much I wanted it. But I think until you're in the thick of it, it's impossible to know how it feels. Early on I know that I got myself typecast as the 'straight talker' of the show and it didn't take long to get boxed in by everything I had created. I was filming stuff that was deep and raw – I got dumped in the *Daily Mail* and on the actual show. How much more raw can you get? Some of the biggest situations of my adult life were there for all to see and I had lost the ability to deal with it as 'me'.

I was trying to be myself, but people had come to expect certain reactions from me, the producers loved it when I found myself involved in other people's drama, and it did get to the point where, if I wasn't naturally involved in it, they would find a way to drag me in. Drama and aggravation followed me everywhere, and when we were filming there was nowhere to go, unless you walked away from the scene, which would have been hugely unprofessional. This was particularly the case as we started my third series in February 2014, and I think it really started to become apparent to me that this cycle could be emotionally difficult to deal with because I was always aware that any reputational damage could affect my long-term career goals.

Off we all went to Mario's and it was my first night back drinking after being dry so it didn't take much to get a bit merry, but not as bad as the others. Mario, Elliott Wright, Tom Pearce and James Bennewith ('Diags') were all there and were winding me up because they had seen me out with Frank, when there had still been some overlap with Charlie. The conversation started with Tom telling me he knew I was cheating on Charlie with Frank, then they all got involved and went for me. I can't lie – I'm the worst liar ever – so when they asked me straight about it I couldn't deny it. They were really harsh and gave me no leeway to reply or defend myself; it was like a pack of wolves quizzing me on everything.

We had all been drinking as we were staying over and didn't have to go anywhere. I'd finished my scenes and so I went to bed. But a few hours later one of the producers came up to get me out of bed and do more filming – it must have been about 3 a.m. because the night was still going on. I wasn't very happy about it and got dressed again, heading downstairs in my blue dress.

I was told to go outside – where I found Charlie glaring at me, clearly fuming. He just looked at me and said: 'Have you got anything to say to me?' He said: 'I know you're seeing someone,' and I disagreed, but you could see I was completely on the spot and not equipped to deal with something so big in the state I was in. It was 3 a.m., I was half asleep and had been given no warning at all. This was my actual life, my ex of three years thinking I'd cheated on him, and all they wanted was their scene.

He went on and said: 'And I know his name is Frank Major.' Now, even though I was half asleep, I did realise Charlie had said Frank's name on screen and that was never allowed unless the person had agreed in advance they were going to appear on the show. I was quite dumbstruck and I walked out of the scene, and that was that until I was then confronted with Frank on the show a few episodes later. They'd brought him on the show and I had to do the most hideous and excruciating scene with him that was directly at odds with all we had discussed when we were together. He had never been interested in the show or the fact I was on it, and yet here we were with him getting his airtime and making me look like a calculating cheat.

We were all staying in the same house, and clever *TOWIE* had put Charlie there too. Obviously I went to Charlie's room to see what was going on and ended up staying there. This was 15 February, and the night before I had been out with Frank for a Valentine's Day meal at Scalini in Chelsea. Frank had dropped me home and nothing had happened. I'd gone off filming and been confronted with Charlie. When I'm in that situation, I revert to pre-*TOWIE* Ferne, the Ferne who only ever needed Charlie and the security of being with him. He always had a way of making me feel that everything would be okay and I needed it that night more than ever.

Anyway, in the morning I did a scene with Gemma and Jess and then had a scene with all the boys. I walked into the kitchen and it was like walking into a firing squad. They went for me and hit me with questions I'd had no idea they were going to ask – you could see from my face. In that situation it is horrendous – what do you do when the scene goes rogue and people start doing things and asking questions you aren't prepared for? If you walk away you aren't doing your job, and if you complain and say you won't do it, the producers simply tell you that you won't get your right of reply. You are screwed either way.

It was the same in a later series, when Gemma came round to Billie's to have it out with me and she told me that no one liked me and accused me of saying she needed a gastric band. That was a total lie and I couldn't do a thing. She had gone rogue and thrown the scene and the producers had let her – again, I felt like the scapegoat. I have to say that since this Gemma and me have made up, she apologised for ever saying that and she remains a supporter of mine and we have each other's backs.

So there I was, admitting to the nation there had been some overlap but that I'd nipped it in the bud right away, which was true. I didn't deserve that stick, and I didn't deserve the way the scene was dumped on me. Those boys who gave me a hard time are the very definition of double standards, given how they've treated girls in the past. Despite what they say, one week of overlap does not define me as a cheat and that scene was very upsetting. I won't lie, I felt a bit thrown to the wolves.

When you know you have a tough scene coming up with someone, it's all about the prep: you can rehearse, rehearse, rehearse, and go through the points with the producers so you're clear what they want you to touch on. Anyone can throw a curve ball – I was expecting drama, but I wasn't expecting Frank sitting there in front of me. I felt really let down.

13

Brand New Experience

It is funny to think that Russell Brand and I would go together in the same sentence in my book, as you couldn't think of two more different people. But actually, our paths have weirdly crossed a lot, the first time when I was just eighteen.

I first met him by chance in 2009 when a group of us all decided to go to one of his gigs – it was his *Scandalous* tour in Brixton. You could argue he was at the height of being famous (maybe infamous might be a better word). The gig was a big highlight – this was when Russell was on tour after the whole Jonathan Ross scandal and he had very much been in the limelight for all the wrong reasons.

We decided to get the train into London and make a night of it, all glammed up and ready for some laughs on our big night out. I was there with Gemma, Sophie, Sam, Billie and their mum, Sue. You know how some nights are so random from start to finish that you look back and wonder if it really can be all in the stars that fate makes stuff happen?

The night didn't get off to the best start when we arrived and realised we had the worst seats in the house, with a massive pillar right in front of us – we could hardly see Russell Brand at all. But the show was hysterical and we had a real laugh, despite our position. Afterwards it was announced that Russell said he would be in the foyer doing photos and signing autographs, so naturally we decided this was too good an opportunity to pass up. Of course we wanted to meet him: we were eighteen and he was huge. We decided to hang about to see what happened. It was heaving with people waiting for a picture, so we decided to take ourselves off to the side and let the crowd calm down a bit. We were sitting there watching the madness when a security guard came over and asked if we wanted to have a drink in the private VIP bar upstairs.

We didn't need asking twice. I do think there is

something about growing up in Essex, and maybe because Billie and me had that job after we left school where we'd met a few famous people: I think we felt much more at home in situations like this one than some girls our age. We very much had the mentality that we would seize our opportunities. It wasn't that we were fame-hungry hangers-on – we were just really curious and adventurous and open to new experiences that came up. You only live once, after all, and if you're not hurting yourself or anyone else, why not?

So up we went to this private bar and the vibe was instantly different. It was full of comedians and a different class of person, more serious and intellectual, I suppose – more like Russell himself. There was a huge long bar and again we took ourselves off to the side to check it all out and see what was what. We were just young girls who'd been given the chance to meet an A-lister and have a picture taken, and that was the extent of what we expected to happen. Danny, his security guard, was at the end of the bar and we got chatting. It turned out Danny was from Billericay, so we traded local stories and got on great – his mum lived near us – and we were having good Essex banter. He told us Russell would be up in a minute and that he would get him to come over.

Now, we might have been eighteen but we weren't stupid. We knew there was every chance this could be their routine: that Russell would send Danny over to chat to the pretty girls and then let Russell know if they were worth bothering with. With that in mind, we were sussing out the vibe when in walked Russell, chatting to everyone and saying hi. It is no exaggeration to say that he lit up the room – it really was as though a bright light went on. I could see instantly that he had an amazing way of making everyone feel special and important. It's such a rare thing and he definitely had whatever 'it' is.

Danny was clearly his partner in crime: he waved him over and told him we had come from Brentwood for the gig and that we were great fun. So Russell came over, and he simply oozed charm and charisma as he asked our names one by one and kissed us hello. He went round the circle we were in very slowly, giving each of us eye contact and time, a total pro. He then said: 'Do you mind if I pull up a chair and join you?' It was all very smooth and we were captivated. He went round the circle again, saying our names to prove he'd remembered them. We chatted about all sorts of stuff and it felt like we sat with

Feeling very *Sex in the City* for my blog.

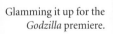

Glamming it up for the *Godzilla* premiere.

Glamour line-up for the
TV Choice Awards.

First Year at the NTAs.

irl Power Shower.

elow: The task I'd
*e*en waiting for.

*e*eling the fear and doing it anyway.

ght: The Eating Challenge – I didn't
*e*xpect the food to still be alive.

One of my favourite shots from my blog.

My first presenting job on *This Morning*.

Right: Me looki
glamourous at *T*
Amazing Spiderma
premiere. I just love t
colour of this dre

This was for the TOWIE calendar and one of my first shoots. I love that it looks so vintage.

This is from this year's NTAs. This was such a great night. It was great being there with everyone from *I'm A Celeb*.

This is me channelling my Riviera look.

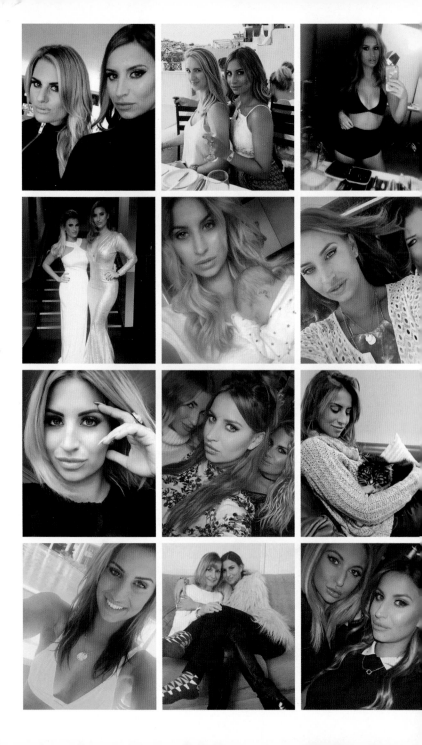

him for about an hour. There was a whole bar full of people there to meet him and not once did he move. There was us, him and Danny.

Eventually Russell said: 'I don't feel like this party should end, girls. Do you want to come back to mine? I mean, Mum, you can come back too, obviously.' Sue immediately said no but told us to stay together and to make sure we didn't stay out all night.

We were very glammed up and ready for a night out after the show – we probably looked a bit over the top, but we didn't let that bother us as we got ready to head back to Russell's. The 'getaway' was all arranged with military precision – the main aim was to avoid the gang of paparazzi outside the club. Russell was obviously hot property, but after all his bad publicity, the press were watching him like a hawk. The last thing he needed was to be spotted with us.

Danny arranged a car to take us back to Russell's. He gave the driver the address, told us to leave the back way and that there would be someone waiting for us at the house to let us in and make us comfortable. Looking back now, I don't know what we were thinking: it was all so cloak and dagger and, if I had a daughter, I'm not sure

I would have been happy at the thought of her in the same scenario, but luckily our mums didn't have a clue!

It was so exciting, we couldn't believe it was happening. We were eighteen, had never really been around a mega-celebrity, and he had picked us to go back to his actual house. We snuck out, avoided the photographers by leaving through the stage door and were bundled straight into the car. As I've said, we were young but we weren't naïve. We discussed the possibility in the car that Russell might be expecting more. He had, after all, just been voted 'Shagger of the Year' – it didn't take a huge leap of imagination to think about what might happen between him and five pretty girls. It wasn't as if there was a massive group going back for a big party; as far as we knew it was just us. All the way there we discussed how surreal the whole thing was and that one of us might end up with Russell. We would wait to see what happened when we got there.

We arrived in the middle of Hampstead Heath in pitch darkness with just the number of his house and nothing else. It was like some weird film set – the house looked abandoned and a bit eerie. We rang the bell and no one was in, then suddenly a guy appeared to let us into this five-storey house, with a basement kitchen that ran the whole length of the house, and a front room that was the entire first floor. I had never seen anything like it in my life. One of the things that stood out the most were the vases of fresh flowers everywhere: they were bird of paradise flowers and they looked stunning. I remember thinking how unusual it was for a man to have a house full of flowers, but as I got to know Russell it became clear that he was anything but usual.

The other thing that really stuck out was that the house was full of West Ham memorabilia. He had a cat called Morrissey, whose food bowls and cat mat were all made out of the football strip – it was hilarious.

There was a moment where I thought: We are in Russell Brand's house and no one knows we're here. What if something happens? But as if by magic, he appeared in the doorway, smiling and friendly and asking if he could get us anything. What I really wanted was a drink, but since he was a recovering alcoholic that was out of the question. Instead we had to make do with a tour of this amazing house. We stopped on the stair to look at a lovely framed drawing – he proudly said: 'Here is a drawing that my dear friend Jonathan Ross did for me.'

What finished me off was that there was a yoga room on the second floor with dozens of ropes hanging down from the ceiling. It was weird enough, but then Russell suddenly jumped up on the ropes and started folding himself into a yoga pose. Here was Russell Brand hanging upside down, mad hair all over the place, eyes closed and humming to himself.

We were running riot: one of the girls was sitting in the enormous bath (fully clothed and without any water in it), one was in the huge bed in the spare room. Then we all got into the Jacuzzi in bras and knickers and the suggestion was there that we all snogged him, which was hilarious. It really was a lot of brilliant banter. We got out of the Jacuzzi and he took us to the top floor and proudly showed us where he did his writing.

That night one thing led to another between us. The others were roaming around downstairs, causing chaos. I have no idea what they were up to, given all there was to drink was tea, but I had other things on my mind. It was the most surreal night of my life, there with Russell in his house, with my mates downstairs going through all his stuff and nosing around his house. It was like some kind of TV soap.

I borrowed a dressing gown and went down to the kitchen. I decided to capture the moment with a snap, which Russell was very happy to do. (Luckily for me, as that picture came in handy a few years later when Russell uttered his famous quote about me: 'I've literally never seen this human.') At the end of the night we decided to head home as it was getting light. As we were getting ready to leave, Russell asked for my number. I gave it to him and genuinely didn't give it another thought.

Billie and me took the next day off from school as we were knackered. She stayed at mine, and when we woke up I turned my phone on and there was a text from Russell. I remember texting the rest of the girls, accusing them of stitching me up and sending a text pretending to be from him as I just didn't believe it. But then when I read it, there was no doubt it was him – it was practically Shakespearean. It was so intellectual I had to google some of the words he'd used. I remember saying to Billie: 'What does one text back to Russell Brand?!'

I replied and we texted throughout the day, but part of me didn't really find it that romantic or exciting, if I'm honest, though the girls thought it was amazing and were desperate for me to go back to his. A few days later I was sitting in Prezzo in Billericay High Street (the glamour!) and my phone flashed up with his name – it was saved under 'Russell B' just in case he texted or called again – and I picked it up. There was still a part of me that didn't expect it to actually be him.

It was just a few days after the gig and he invited me round again – this time offering to send a 'carriage' for me so that I could go back to his for pancakes. In all honesty, I didn't want a repeat performance of the last time and wasn't that into the idea of going round to the house again – I wanted to go out instead. He told me he didn't want to go out and get papped. (He thought it was 'footballer behaviour' – I'm not quite sure why.) He was keener to stay in and cuddle.

He invited me to a gig in Bournemouth and again offered to send a car. I'd recently read a kiss-and-tell story on him from a girl describing exactly what had happened to me – he seemed to have a type and a pattern of behaviour when it came to wooing. In her story, this girl said he'd invited her to a gig and when she got there, there was another girl in the bed with him. I won't lie, I have no clue if any of that was true but it terrified me and put me right off.

But I guess you don't get to be Russell Brand without being persistent. He kept texting. In reality, I think I was a little bit too young and naïve for someone like him;

after a chance meeting at a comedy night suddenly I was being wooed by such a Lothario.

In the end he went off to film *Forgetting Sarah Marshall* in Australia, met Katy Perry and that was that. The last I heard from him was a few months later when I got a new phone and texted everyone in my address book with the new contact details. I signed it off 'Ferne' – he replied immediately with: 'Cotton or Essex?'

Our fling was never really 'revealed', though it was one of those rumours that almost became mythical in terms of the number of people who relived it for me. When it really came back to bite me was at the press conference when I joined *TOWIE* and one of the journalists was trying to work out what my 'Essex credentials' were in order to qualify for the show. One of the interviewers asked me outright: 'Have you kissed a celebrity?'

I was adamant I hadn't and had almost got away with it before good old Arg piped up: 'Er, yeah you have, Ferne – Russell Brand!'

The proverbial cat was out of the bag. Sam went on to write about a 'friend' who'd spent the night with Russell Brand later when she did her book, and everyone put two and two together. It made its way into the press, which prompted Russell to pretend we'd never met. That was embarrassing and a bit hurtful, really, so Sam stepped up and decided to post on Twitter the picture of me in his dressing gown with his arm around me. It was after he'd tweeted:

I've literally never seen this human.

Sam replied to him directly:

You've never seen the person before, really, what's this then?

Although he never replied, he did go on to talk about us in his book *Booky Wook 2*, where we were grudgingly acknowledged. He wrote:

After a night in Brixton Academy I took home five girls and we kissed and canoodled and shrieked till the early morning in my 'never gonna be clean enough' hot tub. And through their white wine kisses I tasted something poisonous.

So fast-forward to 2015, just after I split up with Charlie for the final time. Russell was on his old mate Jonathan

Ross's show and my friend Carl had two tickets to be in the audience for filming. Now, I had never actually sat in the audience at a show before and ITV felt like my home from home because of the *TOWIE* connection, so when Carl asked me, not only did I jump at the chance but I let someone from the production team know and they kindly sorted me out with access to the green room and let us backstage. It was shaping up to be a great night and I was excited. It wasn't until we were there that the line up of guests was revealed. There was Keanu Reeves, Olly Murs, another comedian and Russell! I had no idea he was going to be there.

You know what those shows are like: they record lots of laughter and crowd shots to warm things up and make sure the guests are received properly. Russell has a tendency to walk into the audience and get it going – he likes to meet his fans like that and engage them in what's going on. He was like the Pied Piper, funny and witty, and you could listen to him all day. At the time I was sitting in the audience I was probably at the peak of things in *TOWIE* – there had been non-stop drama and my love life had been aired for all to see, so I was getting a fair amount of stares from some other audience members. I was just praying that Russell didn't come near my section and remember me, as that would not make for a relaxing evening out!

The show was great and we went back to the green room to have one drink. I was intrigued to see if he was there and if he would remember our night, especially given his Twitter denial where he'd seemed keen to ignore the whole thing. It wasn't because I wanted anything to happen, it was more intrigue: there must have been so many women, I simply wondered if he remembered little old me. (He didn't strike me as a potential *TOWIE* fan, so his memory would have to do the job.)

I truly believe that when fate puts you in the path of someone you should do all you can to take advantage of it, but in the end me and Carl got bored with the green room and decided to head to Soho. We slipped out the back of the studios to get a car and, as we came out of the lift, we literally bumped into Russell. He did a double take and I said: 'Hi, Russell. I've met you before.'

He said: 'Yes. Yes, you have,' and grabbed my hand, pulled me to the stairs and looked right into my eyes. We got chatting and I explained that I'd last met him when I was eighteen, and reminded him about going back to his. He was hilarious. He didn't ask me anything much about myself and I told him I worked for ITV. Then it suddenly came back to him and the penny dropped. He shouted: 'You were with the sisters and the mum!'

He was so proud he had remembered and I just laughed as he kept telling me I was beautiful. I remember thinking that he was the sort of man who would understand my look and my vibe. It was as if that same old connection had come back as we stood in the corridors chatting while everyone waited for him to leave. In the end I left with Carl and, sure enough, a few minutes later a text pinged through from him. It was so refreshing that he didn't want to play games – if he likes you he messages.

A few days later I was out and about with the girls in St Paul's and the text banter was back and forth. Russell said he really wanted to see me, but he made me promise that I hadn't been drinking as he couldn't see me if I had been. (I can understand that as he has worked hard to overcome his addiction.) I told him where I was and he said I was so close that I could run to his in a matter of minutes. I was intrigued. Things so far had been so full of near misses – my feeling was that I would never know unless I gave him a go.

I went to his house in east London. He was in bed and

so just buzzed me in and didn't actually get out of bed to greet me. His house was in utter darkness. I called out: 'Russell.' It was so surreal: I was in his house, a virtual stranger, in the pitch dark.

Eventually I found my way to his bedroom. He complimented me on my clothes . . . and then it all went wrong. He made me watch a Stone Roses documentary – twice. Nothing happened, mainly because every time I spoke, he kept telling me to shush because I'd been drinking. I left in the morning feeling horrendous and crap about myself. It was very out of character for this romantic bloke he'd portrayed himself as; the whole time I was getting ready to leave he didn't even really speak to me.

He texted the next day and I replied, saying: 'That went horribly wrong.' I said sorry for having had a drink and we decided to meet up again. There was no denying the chemistry between us when I went back again – we had a great time. And he was so attentive and fun. We saw each other on and off for three months and he showed a sweet and daft side by sending me pictures of myself at the start of my time on *TOWIE*, looking all goofy and daft.

It was one of those dalliances that is a lot of fun but

you know it isn't going anywhere. What did I learn? New words, a love of meditation and the Stone Roses, that there is a lot more to Russell Brand than people think and the realisation that I was ready to do something different. I just wasn't sure what.

14

For Your Entertainment

During the summer of 2014 everything with *TOWIE* really did all come to a head. On the surface I seemed to have fallen out with everyone, even though, ironically, I was one of the ones who got on with everyone when the cameras stopped rolling.

I suppose in many ways this is when the destructive cycle was at its most obvious. I felt suffocated by my TV self, and my involvement in other people's dramas became a weekly occurrence. (One of the things I'm most looking forward to is watching the series when not a cast member, and seeing who is going to pick the rows with who. It isn't easy to stay away from it once you become labelled as someone who provides the entertainment.) It is so easy to knock me and how I've come across and people did, but once you're typecast it's almost impossible to move beyond the person everyone else thinks you are. I think I've tried to explain it earlier, but one of the things that's so hard is that the viewer makes a judgement on you after only seeing an hour of the story. Obviously much more happens off screen and sometimes this can lead to confusion and assumptions being made that aren't always accurate.

Things with Charlie hit an all-time low after Frank Major, and I think, if I'm honest, my love-in with the show started to dwindle from the time Frank was sprung on me in that very awkward scene. I was quite lost and lonely trying to live my life in a certain way within the constraints of reality TV. Life is real, messy and illogical at times, you can't freeze feelings or situations to ensure it demonstrates your best side on the show. That's just not how it works, particularly if you are impulsive and emotional like me. It felt as if the wheels were starting to come off.

Is there anything I really regret? Yes, definitely the row with Chloe Sims in Marbella when we were shooting the summer special in June 2014. Chloe is such a complicated character and so am I, so when we lock heads it's explosive. But I love that girl, she fascinates me and I respect her, so what happened between us hit me very hard and marked a real turning point. After Frank I didn't really know what to do with myself, and I got myself into some situations that weren't ideal, I can see that now.

While we were out in Spain and Charlie and I were enjoying one of our 'on' periods again, there emerged a photo of me in a pool with a guy – I swear on my life that I didn't cheat on Charlie with that bloke, but I know it didn't look good and made Charlie look like a bit of an idiot. I was in a pool in Vegas with my arms wrapped around this boy and was caught by a pap. I had been away with the girls in Vegas and had really let my hair down, had a dance and a drink – but that was it. I had made the most of every minute out there and I genuinely hadn't done anything wrong. I was horrified when those photos emerged during series 12. They looked so bad but I knew the truth: I absolutely had not cheated on Charlie and nothing had happened.

We were in the middle of filming in Marbs. The story broke and Charlie moved out of the villa. It was high drama at a time when I really didn't need any more of it socially, as Charlie and I had been in such a good place.

As I say, it didn't look great, but I swore nothing had happened and it truly hadn't, apart from me massively misjudging the situation. Charlie reacted really strongly and the producers could see the upside for the show, especially as it was all unravelling in the 'now' of the special. With that in mind, the producers wanted to replicate what had happened in real life for the scene – the 'sifting' I mentioned earlier.

So Charlie left the villa and they wanted me to go to the hotel where he was staying so they could capture the reality of what we were going through. That's the point of the show and I used to give that to them all the time. But it is hard when you are the one having the relationship and the cameras can't keep up with your reality. If something happens in your real life you want and need to get it sorted there and then – I mean, when your boyfriend moves out of the villa, you can't wait for the next filming slot!

When we weren't filming and were on down time I got in a cab and went to the hotel where the rest of the cast were; I walked around looking for Charlie as he was ignoring me and not answering my phone calls. It was really difficult having members of the production team creating a barrier between me and Charlie. It was so hard to save it for the scene when all I wanted to do was see him and talk it through there and then. Waiting for the cameras to come on was a nightmare – this was my real life and it was on hold.

I was sent home from the hotel and at times it was hard to know whether this was for my own sake or because the producers wanted to save it for the scene. On my way back to my villa for the final time, I bumped into Chloe. I am sure the producers looked at the situation and put us together. It wouldn't take a genius to work out what would happen when you put me together with Charlie's sister just after I'd been accused of cheating on him, would it?

I will say that these situations were always firmly rooted in what might happen in reality, never outlandishly unlikely. Of course there was every chance I would be wandering around the hotel and could bump into Chloe or Charlie, but it would never have happened like that. They told me I was going to bump into Chloe; I was so angry and frustrated from not being able to talk directly to Charlie about our own relationship that I handled it all wrong. What happened was totally my fault.

She asked me a legitimate question, given that Charlie

was her brother: 'Do you love my brother?' Fair enough, considering what had happened.

'Of course I do,' I said.

We were face to face and we rowed. She called me a slag, and I said: 'You're nasty. Why don't you eat more? You might be nicer!' It was terrible of me to take it personally like that. She had been ill in bed for two days and said that she didn't need this from me. It was unforgivably below the belt, given her past issues. Now, much as I call a spade a spade throughout, if you were to watch all my *TOWIE* scenes back you'd see I was never personal to anyone. I never picked on the way someone looked. Lots of people would comment to me about my nose, but I never retaliated.

Chloe's a fiery girl, she really went for me and, thankfully, a producer stepped in before it could go any further. Immediately I felt terrible and thought: What have I done? I felt total remorse and texted her right away. I am never afraid to say sorry – it has had to become one of my favourite words! I'm the first with an apology, and this has caused me trouble in the past too, as I have a reputation for endlessly apologising and it's led people to think I never mean it. In fact, Chloe was the one who used to say: 'You say sorry all the time. Do you even mean it?' My apologies are always genuine and straight from the heart, I hate hurting people's feelings but sometimes I just angered people. It was bad, and it got me properly thinking about what was real and what was not. But people forget, the show was my job and my life rolled into one. What then followed was a whole series of the show that became my most uncomfortable, and Chloe and I never really got things back on track that whole series. Elliott then became involved and it all descended into a ball of emotions neither of us were given the space to deal with away from the show – that's what made for some of the most explosive scenes.

Things limped along with me and Charlie through the rest of the year. We were off–on and everything in between until we split for good in March 2015. I suppose we were still struggling to find our way post-Marbs 2014 – it became impossible with everyone having an opinion and the rot really set in between him and his family. I know that he hated the whole situation. That boy has never been good with confrontation and, again, this was his relationship with me and with his sister – all the big events in his life being played out for viewers' delight and with no chance to get to the heart of the problem in between filming and real life.

The producers had arranged a scene for Charlie and Chloe to sort out their differences on camera after the long stand-off between the two of them. Charlie was a no-show. The producers brought Frankie Essex back for one episode to console Chloe – and to somehow blame me for Charlie disrespecting his sister by not showing. This actually had nothing to do with me but nevertheless I was blamed. The scene was the final straw for Charlie. He sent me a text after the episode with Frankie had aired, telling me he was done, that the show was toxic on relationships and that I either had to choose our real life or the version the show was making us live.

I got a lot of stick for this: it played into the idea that I was so ambitious I chose the fame over my five-year relationship, but that couldn't have been further from the truth. I knew in my heart of hearts that Charlie and me were done, and I didn't like the way he'd issued me with an ultimatum in Essex-boy style. My God, we'd been through so much. This was not the way to end the most important relationship I'd had, with an ultimatum – 'me or the show' – and certainly not via a text message. I meant what I'd said– the show was my job, I was a professional and I wasn't going to quit my work because I'd had a row with my boyfriend. I didn't know if he would change his mind and want to come back once he'd calmed down. Who knew? It wasn't impossible. What I did know is that his behaviour made me question everything, especially when he tweeted:

> So sad to not lose one . . . But two people you love dearly to a TV show. Everyone can point the finger at me . . . But I have morals. And dignity
> And some sort of self respect. I wish @Chloe_Sims and @fernemccann the best with their lives. But always live knowing you chose the show . . .

He then tweeted his resignation, stating:

> It's time to grow up and move on.

It marked the end of an era and brought out all sorts of feelings that I didn't have time to deal with because we were thrown straight back into the filming schedule. I do see now that I bottled up how I felt, and it all came tumbling out a few months later once we had wrapped up filming that series. It was a dark time.

What also followed was my decision that I needed to keep busy and get fit. I wanted a focus so I decided to join the netball team that my sister had put together. I'd always been passionate about the sport at school, even though I was such an enthusiastic player I sometimes got carried away! The competitive energy of the team was just what I needed and it all came flooding back. (That energy was also a trait that came in massively handy in the jungle.)

It was summer 2015 and we were about to play our first summer league; that means you can pick a name out of a hat and are allowed to play any position. In the first quarter I was goal keeper – not a great running role in terms of keeping fit but I went with it. We played our first match and I jumped up, took a funny turn and rolled my left ankle as I came down. I knew immediately I'd done something terrible – I couldn't get off the court, I was in agony, and my mum took me straight to hospital. It was awful: I had torn two ligaments around my ankle and that was my summer over as far as I was concerned – my first without Charlie and I couldn't even walk. I ended up going back to *TOWIE* in a moon boot and on crutches. By the time all this was sorted it was June, I was filming for the first time without Charlie and I knew I had to go on a trek at the end of August to Machu Picchu in Peru with Lydia Bright. (It was to raise money for CoppaFeel!, which encourages women to check their breasts for early signs of cancer.)

I felt overwhelmed by everything and sank into a depression. I felt so down on myself that I did nothing to help the situation. I didn't take steps to get better – I raged against it instead. Rather than take care of myself and give my ankle the best chance to get better, I went to the Wireless Festival in a moon boot. I was eating crap because I felt so low; I couldn't go to the gym because of my ankle and then compounded it by eating and drinking rubbish. I didn't realise the seriousness of my injury and, to be honest, I didn't care. I was entering a depression and felt like I couldn't do anything to help myself. I was wearing high heels on a catastrophic injury, partying and lacking any focus or direction. I became a soft target for the press, and the final straw was *Daily Mail* pictures of me on the beach in a bikini looking flabby and out of shape.

I have always known deep down that the perfect woman is not real. This whole skinny thing where girls go to the gym for hours every day, it isn't real life, it isn't normal and it isn't how we look. But when you're on a slippery slope, destructive patterns can become familiar and easy. I'm not a size 8, or a nice 5 foot 5 inches, but I do have unusual green eyes and nice skin, so I had always been able to concentrate on the good parts and used to tell myself there is only one Ferne McCann – no one else can be her. I was always confident and sure of who I was, but after my ankle all that went out the window.

At one point I told my manager I didn't want to go anywhere, see anyone, do anything, and I wouldn't leave the house. I got her to cancel all my PAs as I felt disgusting. I didn't even want to post any pictures on Instagram – I couldn't look at myself.

I do feel a lot of pressure to post those pictures looking all happy and it's hell when you feel like crap. It can be exhausting having to appear to be living the dream and be on message when your world is crumbling round you and you feel worthless. Looking after the brand is part of my job, but I find it hard to be authentic if I don't really feel it. It is my life, at the end of the day, not some endorsement advert. It all felt out of control.

I was newly single and things were spiralling. I was attracting lots of boys who weren't good for me and I had a permanent feeling of sadness inside of me. I would spend two hours a day lying on my mum's bathroom floor, scrolling through Instagram, looking at beautiful girls (trust me, this is not recommended if you are feeling down on yourself, it does not make you feel better: far from it). I felt awful; I was on *TOWIE* but everyone hated me, and I felt fat and ugly because I had to wear that awful boot. I would spend time looking at other people's lives and got myself into such a spiral that I probably wasn't pleasant to be around. I didn't want to be with Charlie but I missed the security. I didn't know if any of what I was doing on the show was worth it – I felt hated and misunderstood.

It got so bad that I sat down with Daniella and Andrew, who were the execs at the time: I met them in a hotel with my manager, on neutral ground, and I told them how unhappy I was. It was probably one of the most honest conversations I've ever had. It came after the issues with Chloe, and Elliott throwing a scene and saying I had asked to have sex with him in the toilets. I had an overwhelming feeling that people were trying to throw me under the bus for their own sakes and that I'd become an easy target. People had started to treat me like a punchbag and I was so very tired of feeling like this and being portrayed like this.

I wanted to leave. I had tried to keep out of other cast members' aggravation and yet they still came at me. It wasn't working and it wasn't worth it. That shiny dream of fame I'd had at the beginning of my time on the show wasn't worth feeling like this, I knew that. The public hated me and I wasn't getting any benefit from it and I wanted to go. Without trying to sound too dramatic, I felt done in by it all.

From that conversation, the producers promised me a whole restyle button, to wipe the slate clean. They promised to keep me away from aggravation that didn't involve me (but I did still put my foot in it!). My scenes became lighter and showed my fun side. The last series with Gatsby (Liam Blackwell) was one of my favourites and one I will remember so fondly. It was just so nice not to be screaming and crying all the time and not to have people in my face calling me out on things that had nothing to do with me. My last proper series was the perfect way to end things. I am so glad that I didn't leave back in the summer of 2015 – it allowed me to leave in a good place and feeling fond of the show. I look back now and I do feel sad about the fact that I'll never have that again, but in the end it was right.

I went to Machu Picchu with Lydia for CoppaFeel! and it was one of the best things I've ever done. Lydia was the perfect girl to go with. She is such a great girl and so real and emotional. (She cried every night in our tent just from being in such an amazing environment – she lived and breathed it and I loved that about her.) It was a crazy time. We didn't wash for five days, just a little brush-down with a face wipe was the best we could do. We had our feet in buckets of water, we were exposed to the cold and the snow, the wind and the rain at all times – any extreme you can imagine, we experienced it.

When it got to actually climbing the mountain, around 1,500 steps and with a ridiculous incline, that was the crowning moment for me. It was the toughest thing I have ever done (even tougher than the jungle), and I got up that mountain second, out of twenty people. I was actually crawling up on my hands and knees. I got to the top and I know it might sound like a cliché, but I saw the whole world in front of me and it took my breath away. I had a moment where I realised the world was incredi-ble – I had been so busy in self-destruct mode that I'd forgotten to celebrate all that was good about my life. I experienced a deep sense of calm and gratitude that I hadn't felt for a very long time and, at that time, life felt good.

I'd had my moment with nature and felt as though I'd recaptured something in myself that had been missing. The chat I'd had with the producers had given me something to hold on to and had made me realise that I had to get myself on track. I could choose to be positive or I could sabotage it; I wanted to feel happy again more than anything.

I decided to go and see someone – not a therapist or anything like that, but a healer. I went to see someone called Carol and she completely changed my life and how I look at things. She got to the heart of my insecurities and made me realise that part of the problem is the fact that I'm not as self-confident as people think, but that I put myself under a huge amount of pressure to appear in control. It is as though I have a self-destruct button in me, where I am full of anxiety about losing everything I've worked for, so I sabotage it for myself.

Injuring my ankle was a huge deal and I had to accept that I don't and won't look or feel the same – it is a completely different shape. Every time I look down at my ankle it's a little reminder of what the universe felt I needed to know. I believe the injury and the depression were all part of what I had to go through to get me ready for my biggest adventure yet: the Australian jungle.

15

That's a Wrap

I f Gemma Collins was to be believed, there was zero chance of anyone from *TOWIE* getting on *I'm a Celebrity . . . Get Me Out of Here!* in 2015. She said the show was moving away from all that and looking for a different type of celebrity.

It did make some sense, as *TOWIE* had been well represented on the show over the past few years. They'd had Mark Wright, Joey Essex, Gemma Collins – why would they take a fourth *TOWIE* person in a row when there were other shows to explore? Also, a lot of the cast thought that Gemma might have mucked it up for all of us by behaving the way she did in the jungle when she was there. Though Gem had her reasons for leaving the show.

Life had been a hamster wheel for me and something needed to change. I felt good that I'd had the chat with the *TOWIE* producers and things were, hopefully, taking a new direction, and I was keen to explore other avenues regarding TV. I have a great manager, Leisa, who has been a breath of fresh air for me. There is no better feeling than knowing that the person representing you believes in you 100 per cent and wants the very best for you. I would be lost without her but, most of all, she has given me great confidence to go out there and undo the perception that people have of me. It has sometimes felt like an uphill struggle, but we've tried to take it a step at a time and, as I said earlier, I'm a great believer in the fact that being yourself wins in the end – your true self is all you have.

After that dark spell and the meeting with Daniella and Andrew from *TOWIE*, I had a real shift in perception. Suddenly I knew what I wanted and it was like I knew who I was again. So me and my manager set out a clear strategy and set of goals. Of course there were things on that list that seemed out of our control but we both believed it would happen with hard work and clear focus. Top of the list was a big TV show. We did lots of meetings with various bookers and heard about all sorts of great new shows as well as the established ones. In the back of my mind I knew I really wanted to do *I'm a Celebrity . . . Get Me Out of Here*! but there was this niggling memory of Gemma saying they weren't looking for *TOWIE* people this year. Plus it was such a massive show I imagined I would be up against all sorts of household names – I knew plenty of people who would have done anything to get on it. But, as strange as this may sound, I still had a feeling it was going to happen and I would get on the show.

After auditioning for a couple of the key shows, I was offered one. I was so excited but then realised it clashed with my Machu Picchu trek; I had committed to that and there was no way I would let them down. I was gutted at first, but we just ploughed on with our strategy and the more positive I became about things and the more I believed, the better things were becoming. I worked so hard: when I say we created opportunities, we really did. I am not frightened of hard work, the busier I am the better. One of my best sayings is 'the harder I work the luckier I get'.

It was 2015 and Halloween was on the horizon and we were filming a party, all dressing up and getting into the spirit. Billie came to mine to get ready and it was like our teenage years again – all blaring music, make-up and chat. We were running late, Billie had to drop Nelly off at her mum's and I was late back from an appearance – it was action stations. I really hate getting ready in a rush, but we didn't have long until our cars came.

As we tried to get sorted, my phone was ringing off the hook: it was my manager, Leisa. I picked it up and explained that we were running late, I was stressed – could we speak later? She was adamant that I would want to take five minutes to speak to her there and then. So I took the phone into my mum's room and asked what was going on.

She told me that she'd had an email from David Harvey, the booker from the *I'm a Celebrity . . . Get Me Out of Here!* team. They wanted to talk to her about the possibility of booking me for the show. I met them the next day. I was in absolute shock.

I didn't tell a soul. After all the disappointment, there was no way I was going to do anything that might compromise it. I filmed the Halloween party, and then the next morning we had the meeting. I was so wound up and nervous – desperate for the chance to do something so amazing. But afterwards I was convinced I'd messed it up, that I hadn't been myself. I came out deflated and disappointed in my performance. The previous meetings had left me feeling confident that I had done my best; with this one I didn't even feel I'd been talking like myself. I think I'd just wanted to impress so much that everything else had taken over.

The interview had been very thorough – they'd asked questions like: 'What are your fears? What are your good and bad points? Who would you least like to be in there with?' and some generic questions, too, about likes and dislikes. The psychology of how they asked the questions was interesting: they would ask a question and then sit back and let me speak, never interrupting. There was no two-way interaction, so I never really knew when to stop talking and I can see that it would be very easy to dig yourself into a hole with it all. You know how it is: once you start, it can be hard to know when to wrap it up. It was the opposite to the other interviews I'd had, where they would stop me and change direction, ask another question in a different way. It had been very interactive and quite detailed.

Anyway, I came out and I just felt as if I'd completely mucked it up. The next morning Leisa and I were at my house with my mum when Leisa's phone rang. I felt sick. So, in a matter of just two days, I got an email and a phone call saying they wanted to meet me, and then the day after that they called to confirm they wanted to book me! It was that quick. I can actually still hear him say the words: 'We would love to book Ferne.' I don't think I will ever forget them.

I collapsed in tears, completely overwhelmed. It was that sense of finally having been accepted and, in this case, by a show I loved and respected. I couldn't believe they wanted me, after believing for so long that no one liked me and that there was nothing I could do to change that, no matter how hard I tried to justify the real me. To hear those words – 'We want her' – gave me the best feeling in the world. It was like nothing else and I knew how life-changing those words were going to be; this was the start of something so exciting and I was raring to go.

I was caught up in a total whirlwind and was swept off my feet by the excitement and speed – it all happened so fast! I was asked to interview for the show on 31 October and flew out to Australia on 13 November, my mum's birthday. Obviously it was 100 per cent confidential – more than anything else I had ever done, it had to stay top secret. Apart from Mum and my sister Sophie (who I would trust with my life), I didn't tell a soul. Right before I went out and the rumours had started that I might be in it, I told a very good friend (not part of the *TOWIE* scene). She has her own nail business and has become my go-to nail person. When I told her, we both cried as she did my pedicure because we couldn't believe it was finally happening for me. That was a lovely moment, and the moment that it dawned on me that this was *really* going to happen. The shock lasted for a very long time.

These things never stay secret for long – the media start digging around to see what they can find out, hoping to be the first to expose who might be getting on that plane to join the camp. As a viewer it's always part of the fun to speculate who's going in, and now mine was one of the names being thrown around. So by the time I went out to Australia it had been in the papers that it was me. Most of the contestants had already flown out, so the information lockdown wasn't as vital.

It now seems so fitting that the finale of *TOWIE* series 16 was Nanny Pat's eightieth birthday celebration; it was the perfect way to honour that amazing matriarch of the show. She was a total legend, and I really believe *TOWIE* was all the better for having had her. She will be so missed. Although I didn't know it at the time, it was to be my last series too – what an honour to leave the show at the same time as Nanny Pat filmed her last scenes. So there we were at her glamorous party, I was saying my goodbyes and getting ready to fly off. At that point I had every intention of coming straight back to the show and just saw it as a short break.

Most people were very happy for me, although I did sense a touch of jealousy from some of the other cast members. Maybe that's just a natural response for some people. There had been rumours that Chloe had been in the running for the 'reality slot' on *I'm a Celebrity* and that, for some reason, it hadn't quite come off. Obviously that slot was my slot and, given our up-and-down history, I'd been worried about her finding out. If the rumours were true and the gig had nearly been hers, then that would be awkward and hard for her to deal with. Do you know something? She could not have been nicer or more generous about it all and she was genuinely happy it had come off for me. It was funny because, when I got to the jungle, I would often have a moment sitting in my hammock, thinking to myself of all the people who would love to be right there in my shoes. I never took for granted that I'd been given one of the hottest reality gigs on TV, and loads of people would have killed for it. But it was tough, make no mistake, it's not for the faint-hearted.

My last scenes on *TOWIE* ended up being with Gatsby and Billie. We were drinking to Nanny Pat and we were all glammed up for the party; it all felt quite mellow and nice. Then the producers decided things needed mixing up a bit, so they called over Jake and Chloe. My heart sank, as I knew they would want some kind of 'scene' – it was the finale and some characters like to 'go out on a high'. I just thought: Here we go . . .

So over they came and immediately started trying to get a rise out of me – not helped by the fact we'd had a falling-out earlier in the day. In a way it was exactly what I was used to and perhaps what people had always believed I was guilty of, being too straight up in the scene and going in too hard. In this case it felt obvious to me that they hadn't put the incident to bed and wanted to carry on the argument. I knew that feeling well – if you didn't feel you could draw a line under it then it became hard to leave it at the door, especially when the people you'd been rowing with were in the same scene. It was another instance of the show set-up making it hard to keep perspective or nip things in the bud.

It felt as though they started to pick at me. This time, however, I just refused to rise to it, even when Jake looked at me and said: 'What is wrong with your actual face?'

and 'What are you going to do about that nose of yours?' I didn't even really feel angry with him; if anything, I felt sorry for him. I could remember a time when it'd all used to get to me so much too, when I would live and breathe it all and become completely entangled in everyone else's emotional drama.

All I wanted before I flew off was a nice little scene with Billie and Gatsby. I am so happy I didn't let that final time on set become negative. When I didn't bite, it became clear that the producers must have been expecting a different response from me and asked us to do the scene again. I just didn't want to rise to it and was fed up with being seen as the reactionary one. In the end they cut the entire scene. After spending so long at the heart of all the tears and tantrums, aggravation and drama, my final scene was perfect and brilliantly rounded off my whole experience on the show.

As I said, I had no idea that would be it for ever on *TOWIE*. In a way it took a while for that fact to settle in – being in the jungle and then coming back was nonstop; I think it was only three months on that I got a chance to process it all. I've had to look at it like any job, really. You make both friends and colleagues, and when you move on, you keep the friends close to you and leave the colleagues behind. That's the point: being friends with colleagues only really works when you can talk about work; real friends means you can talk about anything. I still love my mates from that show with all my heart and I think, despite everything, most of them wished me well. I can see now that leaving had to happen for my sanity. I was lucky enough it was for something so amazing.

I felt in a good place and calm – the perfect state of mind to travel halfway around the world and face a whole new challenge that would change my life for ever.

16

I'm a Celebrity Get Me Right in There

I finished filming and had exactly one week to prepare for the biggest thing in my life. People often ask if I did much research. Not really is the honest answer, but mainly because I didn't need to. I'd watched every single series of *I'm a Celebrity . . . Get Me Out of Here!* and can proudly say I had never missed an episode. What I did do though, was to google which bikinis previous female contestants had worn (high-end research indeed!).

The first step to get through was my psych test and there was also a medical, which was another hugely secretive part of the build-up. It's a full-on day and also includes getting publicity photos done wearing your jungle outfits after you've been correctly sized up for

241

clothes and boots. A soon as I put those boots on, it all started to feel very real.

The psych test was fairly straightforward with no hidden surprises. I hadn't really been sure what to expect, so I went pretty much prepared for anything as it was the first time I had experienced anything so extreme.

Initially I didn't have a date for flying out and that made me incredibly nervous – in my mind couldn't help but worry that maybe it was all a dream and I wasn't really going after all. I kept having a nightmare that they might not actually put me in the camp and that they might change their minds – all of those old insecurities surfacing again. The other big fear I had was that they would keep me out of the original main camp, so I would end up being part of a group that they parachuted in halfway through the series to disrupt the status quo. That's one thing about being part of the reality side of the TV industry: you always have a much better understanding of what might go wrong and, in some cases, how you might be used and misinterpreted. There is always the fear after having been on a show like *TOWIE*, that people will think they can use you any way they like, sometimes at your expense. Don't get me wrong, I knew the jungle wasn't like this, but my mind was in overdrive and all scenarios were entertained.

Obviously one of the main concerns was who was going to be sitting round the campfire with me. Before I flew over, I had become aware that there was lots of chat about Vicky Pattison going on to the show and that was sort of confirmed when Pete Wicks and Danielle Armstrong saw her out at the leaving party she threw just before she set off for Australia. So one by one, details were released about who was going in and off they flew. In a way it was great for me as I was still in the UK with full access to all the press, so I could see how the camp was shaping up far more than anyone out in Australia could. Once you land you're put straight into lockdown from every outside influence: family, media, friends, you are cut off from it all.

Then I got the call telling me I was going in three days. I didn't know what that meant in terms of camp dynamic and they didn't give me any more details; all they said was not to worry as, when I did go in, it would all be about me. It sounded exciting and ominous all in one, and I still didn't know the complete line-up as it stood, except that there might be thirteen of us instead of the usual twelve.

The day I was flying I called my mates and said my

goodbyes. I spoke to Danielle and Jess, who'd been out in Chelsea the night before and had bumped into Jamie Laing and Spencer Matthews from *Made in Chelsea*. They got chatting, and Spencer hinted that he was flying the next day. My mind went into overdrive: Vicky had thrown a leaving party and flown to Australia but still hadn't entered camp with the rest; I was flying that day and Spencer the following one. Suddenly it all made sense: they were holding us three back to do a 'reality TV' group with us. They were taking the three most successful reality shows and, from within those shows, three of the most outspoken personalities, and they were going to have a lot of fun.

Now, on paper that was all well and good, but I was nervous, particularly about Vicky. Obviously I had the Charlie situation in the back of my mind. The pictures of her and Charlie had hurt, they'd rubbed salt into the wound, and then to read in her book that he'd spoken to her about us, negatively, at a time I'd thought we were happy – that was hard too. That was on him, not her, but I did bring it up in my column in *Star Magazine* at the time to address it and then hadn't really bumped into her since. So while it wasn't a huge deal, the potential for awkwardness was there. The perception of her was that she was outspoken and a bit upfront but, given everything I'd been through over the years, I was going to be the last person to cast stones. One saying I live by and always will is that you should never judge a book by its cover. At times I have longed for people to extend the same kindness to me, and I certainly wasn't going to judge the girl before I'd met her properly. Take as you find, I say.

When it came to Spencer, I'd only seen him once and I won't lie, he hadn't been the most friendly person I'd ever met. But there had been no big drama: we'd just been out and about and said a quick hello. Now I had sussed the plan out, I immediately worried that, as there were three of us from similar situations and we would be one extra, they would make us compete against each other and only two of us would actually get to go in. I kept saying to Leisa that they were probably going to get rid of one of us. I just felt it was too good to be true for me and something was bound to go wrong.

With all of that swirling around in my head I got on the plane and had the longest flight ever – I stopped in Dubai and Singapore so that the producers could keep me away from Spencer, who was also on his way out there just a few hours behind me. When we finally landed in Australia I felt exhausted, excited and scared all in one. I wandered through the airport and it was dead – not a single person to be seen. It was quite a lonely feeling; even though I was ready to embrace whatever came next, I was very far from home.

You know what it's like with long flights, you lose all sense of reality and time goes out the window. I was eating dim sum at what should have been my UK 4 a.m. and had no idea what was going on. I was met at the airport by security. Everyone is immediately given their own chaperone – that person stays by your side at all times. And as soon as you land you go into lockdown – there is an immediate blackout on you seeing anything, talking to anyone and reading anything. Basically, it's like being in captivity and you leave the outside world.

The show's producers find a different hotel for every single contestant, so in our case, that was thirteen different hotels at the same time. If they stagger the entrance of the contestants, it means everyone has different lengths of time in lockdown, for example Vicky had a whole week and I had four days. That meant four days of asking my chaperone permission to do anything at all – going outside, you name it, I had to ask permission. By my second day there everything relaxed a bit and I was allowed to wander about, get some lunch and sunbathe.

I was lucky to get on so well with my chaperone too, you can't help but bond with them.

By the second day, things kicked off – there was a press day and a photo shoot and suddenly it was all action stations. Everything was confiscated – they take away your phone, iPad, laptop; anything you have that allows you to keep in touch with the outside world is removed. Rumour has it not everyone complied though: supposedly clever Duncan Bannatyne took in two phones and put one in his suitcase. The producers don't search you, but the idea is that you aren't supposed to take in more than one device, that they then keep until you leave the camp.

I finally went in on the third episode and it wasn't really what I'd been expecting, as we entered the camp wearing our everyday clothes and hadn't been given our jungle uniform. I had no idea what was happening or what time of day it was as you travel everywhere in these blacked-out trucks, which makes it impossible to know how far away anything is or where on earth you are. I got in the helicopter and it landed in the middle of the jungle; I jumped out and there was a film crew to capture the moment as soon as I stepped on to the ground. It is literally in the middle of nowhere – remote doesn't even cover it. (It's funny how people who don't know anything about the show will joke that there must be a hotel round the corner. Er, no!)

That first day was a long one that started as soon as we were dropped off. My boots and socks were there waiting for me, and then we just had to sit around for hours in little tents, waiting for instructions. We waited for any kind of information and initially were told it would only be twenty minutes until we went off. But it was hours, mainly because there was only one crew who had to film everything and as we were being brought in one at a time it was taking for ever.

Eventually we were off and were taken straight to Snake Rock by lantern light, where I met Vicky and Spencer. The whole way there I still couldn't believe I was in the jungle! When I met the other two, we bonded straight away and chatted and we were all on a level. I had built it up in my mind and decided that we would be walking into a head-to-head trial, perhaps for a place in the camp or perhaps for food, who knew? But I had a feeling it would be harsh whatever it was. I knew we weren't going into the main camp because it was so late but I had no idea what they would do with us.

I was terrified and it was pitch black and freezing; the first thing we needed to do was light the fire. It was clear from the beginning that camp life was very much about taking the initiative. But what you see is what you get: all we had was our swags. They call you in to give you basic instructions but you are on your own. The first thing we did was get the fire on as it was freezing.

There was only rice and beans that hadn't been cooked, and you obviously have to boil the water before you can drink it, so things were better once the fire was sorted, though it did take us a while to light it. You have lanterns that stay on until you go to bed, then they dim but stay lit so you can make your way around. Snake Rock is tiny and there is a dunny in the corner and that's kind of it. We had no idea how long we'd be there for, why we were there or what the plan was, but we knew we'd be spending the night and were certain we would have to complete a trial for our supper.

It is so hard to explain what it is like in there and how surreal it feels. You never see a single member of the crew unless you're leaving the camp to do a trial – it is like a weird no man's land.

We all got changed and there were laminated instructions telling us we had a trial first thing. I was so taken with the moment that I suggested a team hug. It just seemed a good thing to do given that we were getting on so well – it was as if we had known each other for ages. What we didn't see was Ant and Dec go into the main camp and deliver the news that none of the existing campmates had to do the trial. They were partly relieved, and then partly agitated as they were told that they had three new campmates there in Snake Rock to do it instead.

So the three of us had to do the trial and were told that the winner would move to camp. I later heard from Lady C that no one wanted us in there because they'd heard who we were and thought we were awful. We were all good with each other, though, and had bonded immediately over the whole 'reality' thing. People thought we would compete with each other but actually it wasn't like that; it was a respect for the shows we were on and how hard we worked. I genuinely liked Vicky and Spencer and was so happy they were with me in that first bit while we got used to things.

As we geared up for the trial, my biggest fear was that I would be the weakest link of the threesome. In a way I was, as those other two were fearless in that first task – they smashed it. We went off to do the trial and had no idea if we would be going back to Snake Rock, going to the main camp or just going home.

The whole night before the trial, we were all banging on

about how we would be in it together. Then we heard that we would be head-to-head and I felt sick. Vicky and Spencer hit it off right away – I think there was a real spark there from the minute they met – and they kept reassuring me it would be okay. Anyway, the day dawned and off we went to do the trial called Dicing with Danger.

I just want to make it clear: despite the front I put on, I hated the trials and that first one was murder. I know they thought I would pull out when they put a snake in the box and it started biting me. I just lost it big time. The cockroaches stank to high heaven and I was having a terrible time. When they put the snake in I remember screaming, 'It's touching me!' and 'What if it goes in my nose?!' I immediately established myself as the one who made funny noises and screamed – though believe me, there have been noisier contestants in the past. I couldn't help it though, I made grunts like I was in labour. My hands were pressed so tightly against the sides of the perspex box as they dropped in the snakes.

Ant and Dec were cracking up. I have to say, I love those boys. They make the show what it is and are just lovely to be around, even if you are eating crocodile testicles!

Don't ask me how but I won the first task, as it was all about the luck of the dice. As my reward I got to pick either Vicky or Spencer to take with me. I don't think I even hesitated before I said: 'Sorry, Spence!' I took my girl with me. It was no competition as I knew he would be okay. There was not even a choice to make, no way was I leaving her there on Snake Rock on her own.

I've always had quite good radar and I think you can pick up on someone's energy from the very moment you meet them. To my mind, from the off, the people who were nicest were Jorgie Porter, George Shelley and Brian Fried-man (which was unfortunate as we had to banish two of them pretty much straight away). We hadn't even taken off our backpacks when we were called up to the BT to collect the latest task. Ours was to immediately banish two people to Snake Rock so that there would be room for us to join the camp. Those two people would exist on basic rations of rice and beans; they would be joining Spencer, who we believed would want positive and upbeat people. Jorgie was both of those things and had been instantly lovely. It might sound a bit weird to banish her for her upbeat nature but, in our heads, it made complete sense. She didn't strike me as someone who would get the hump either, unlike Duncan, who I suspected would not be happy if we sent him away and would let everyone know it. In the end we sent Brian, as we thought he was the sort of guy who would thrive in any environment (though I did suspect he wouldn't be too chuffed).

Vicky and I are similar in some ways, but Vicky was feistier than me and I'm actually quite laid-back about stuff – this came out immediately as Vicky and I decided who should leave the camp. It was tough going in later than the others. Imagine school starting in September and everyone making friends and you arrive in November and have to try to fit in. In the camp, a few days makes a lifetime of difference and everyone has already decided who is good at what and what the cliques are. In this case the jungle clique was made up of Susannah Constantine, Yvette Fielding, Brian, George and Jorgie. All the rest were doing their own thing. She may have been in the clique but Susannah was so lovely from the outset, kind, fun and the mother of the group; she definitely looked out for us and I was gutted she left the camp so early on.

Initially it was hard to get a grip on the dynamic of the camp as people were in and out so much. The first few episodes I was in involved the main camp competing against Snake Rock, so that involved pulling people over and then giving them the chance to win back their place in the main camp. At any one time I think the maximum number of people at Snake Rock was five – Brian, Jorgie, George, Yvette and Susannah – when we went head-to-head for the task. Once the task was completed and they came back, I remember there was a moment where I thought: this could become interesting and tricky as they seemed to have bonded, like they were determined to keep their tight group together.

I was sitting on my hammock and the clique were lying on Yvette's bed, just having come back, and they quite loudly started to discuss how people were about to start getting voted out. One of them said to the others: 'We need to keep this tight,' and gestured with their index finger in a circle that went round the group sitting on Yvette's bed. It was clear Vicky and I were always going to be the new girls, no matter how long we were there. This might have been when the viewers got their first glimpse I wasn't who they thought I was. I think those *TOWIE* fans out there would have expected 'fiery Ferne from *TOWIE*' to overhear something like that, stand up and start shouting the odds – 'I can hear that! What do you mean?' type of thing, getting all uptight and angry. But that isn't me, and this – and so much else – just went over my head. They aren't the sort of things that upset me in real life. It wasn't that I was playing a game and trying to be a version of myself that people would like. It was simply me, and the real me didn't care.

We were allocated chores every day by the camp leader and everyone thought I was mad because I loved my to-do list, just adored the routine, and it was a great way to pass the time. I can hand on heart genuinely say that I never got bored in there, not once. Getting ready was a chore in itself because it was impossible to ever get clean. I know people might have thought that a glammed-up Essex girl would have struggled massively in there, and some would have, I'm sure, but to me it took me right back to my carefree tomboy days of spicy clothes and old, worn jumpers. I loved it. There was no mirror, so you had to use the reflection of the telephone box mainly, but sometimes I would go and do my hair in the BT, as I was able to look into a camera and big screen and get a better view of my whole face.

Washing was tricky as you couldn't ever get naked, so you never really felt clean, but everyone gets a pack before they go in with all the same toiletries inside and one luxury item. So in the pack we had: roll-on deodorant that smelt of citronella that I used as perfume, hand sanitiser, shaving balm, a razor, toothbrush, dental floss, toothpaste, moisturiser in a bottle, sun cream and insect repellent. There were also huge bottles of shampoo and conditioner left by the shower. You are constantly dirty, but I was in my element and I think we all just accepted that it was a part of the experience, like one long festival. (There was a period of time where Duncan didn't shower for three days and that was hard for the rest of us!) At the start there is so much faff as you try to get showered and dry without showing your body etc.; by the end I could do it one-handed.

The uniform was fairly basic so I liked to add my own spin to it. With so much time on my hands out there I did get creative; one thing I did was to invent the jungle skirt. For the uniform you were given two vests, two T-shirts, two pairs of red shorts, one pair of red trousers, two pairs of socks, two shirts, one jacket. I hated the shorts and the trousers; even though I'm quite a tomboy I didn't feel good in them at all, so I improvised. I took one of my T-shirts and, using the knife, Brian sliced the top off so it was off-the-shoulder, and then I tied it. So I wore that over my vest that I pulled down into a skirt and then I tied the spaghetti straps into my bra so it was like a proper little skirt and T-shirt. Then we had a belt that had a buckle and I made it into a choker.

The routine in there was comforting, though there

was no concept of time. I think viewers at home forget that it's live and that, when Ant and Dec would come down to do the eviction during the show, we had actually all just woken up! At the start of the show when they roll the titles and scream 'Get me out of here!', we could hear that in camp and that would be our nod to get up. They would wake us up at about six thirty so we could be round the fire eating breakfast at the end of the televised show to hear who would be doing the trial that day. When it came to going to bed, we would all turn in pretty much at the same time and we were all always so tired. I had the best sleep of my life out there and I was one of only two who chose to sleep in a hammock. There were five camp beds and five hammocks. When we arrived later than the rest it was just a case of fitting in where the rest of the camp would let us, but coming in after everyone had unpacked was tricky as I didn't feel I had my own space or bed area. People often ask if you sit around the fire talking until all hours and the answer is no because you are too tired. It is hard to explain the exhaustion you feel, it is so tiring you can't wait to get to bed. All those shots of people lying in hammocks chatting are when dinner is being made, not late at night gatherings – we all slept as soon as we got into our sleeping bags.

The producers have to watch you all the time in case a deadly snake gets you, and the BT is open at all times. That's not the only weird change I experienced to my daily routine – my new daily diet instantly made me feel fantastic. The main thing was that I didn't drink in there. The whole month I was there, I had two glasses of champagne with my final meal and one drink at the banquet. The diet was amazingly fresh: no salt or seasoning, no sugars, no wheat, so combined with the no booze I genuinely don't remember a time when I felt so good. It wasn't just a food detox either, it was like a retreat from life – I had no phone, no stress, no social media. They were simple times and I think, after the madness of the previous year, it was just the best thing to happen to me. I lost weight, I felt healthy, stress-free and happy in my own skin, and that hadn't happened for a long time.

I am a natural worrier and obviously I did experience anxiety about how the public would react to me. After all that I'd experienced it isn't a surprise. I would talk to the faceless voice at the BT about my anxieties and they would say: 'Ferne, you need to relax.' That faceless voice got me through some moments of self-doubt. It's an amazing set-up and so many talented people have a big role in making it the huge success it is. Part of the anxiety was bound up in the fact that I kept getting voted for trials. It is so hard to know if it is because the public like you or because they don't, but more of that later.

Behind the scenes is fascinating. Camp is exactly as you see it on TV, though perhaps a bit more intense and smaller than you would think. We'd all sit around the fire but what you don't see is the massive canopy that covers the entire main camp area and that looks like a hot air balloon. It's designed to keep you dry in downpours (though it doesn't as the rain comes in the sides and my hammock was right on the edge and I got soaked!). The food comes in a bag on a zip wire and is sent down automatically. The only time you have crew in the camp is if you're leaving, though you do see scenes of celebrities talking to the crew and sharing fears about tasks and they do speak to you when your mic packs are changed.

I just threw myself right into the whole thing. Although I was keen to show people another side, I didn't go into the jungle desperate to make people like me; I went in mainly because it was the experience of a lifetime and I love the outdoors. I knew it was an amazing opportunity and it had the added bonus of allowing me to properly live the outdoors life. I was full of gratitude for the fact that I could be one of thirteen people picked to do it. It was an overwhelming experience and I felt so lucky and free.

This did mean that I didn't have time for any moaners who complained about missing home. There was one scene in which Yvette was going on about how much she wanted to go, and crying when she didn't get voted out, and I said: 'Go then.' It wasn't as out of the blue as it seemed: it had come after days of her not being particularly nice to me. I tried hard with everyone and they all gave back, apart from Yvette. We would sit around the fire and I would ask her questions about how she got into showbiz or ask her to tell a ghost story, and she would say: 'Do I have to do it now?' She made it hard to find a way in and was quite a drain on morale. She did warm up a bit after Susannah and Brian had left – I suppose she had no choice really. We had a few moments where I did her hair round the fire, but overall I didn't feel she welcomed us with open arms. I always had a feeling she didn't like me and Vicky and I realised I was right when she accused us of game-playing in her interview when she came out. My attitude was that while we were in there, we all wore the same clothes and were all equal – a bit like prison in that way.

Duncan was hilarious – the classic grumpy old man but loads of fun too. He would really make me laugh and we had a love/hate relationship as he was quite lazy when it came to the jobs. Towards the end I found that whatever I would do, he'd have something to say about it and that did start to wind me up. It got to the point where if I lit a candle, up would pipe his voice: 'Why're you lighting a candle?'

He questioned everything and that was our relationship. There was one time he annoyed me and it was after the task where I had been stuck in a tunnel, in the rain, covered in rotten fruit. That was also the night I was on cooking duty and probably the one really down day I had. I just had the hump. It was also the day that Lady C came back with no stars so we just had rice and beans, which isn't very rewarding as a chef. Anyway, Jorgie and I had done the task and had had a terrible time. I'd cooked and we just didn't have the energy to wash up so we left the dishes in the camp – everyone was fine with that. Then we decided to do it but didn't dry it up or put it away in the pantry.

When I woke up the next morning, I opened my eyes to find a plate in my face and Duncan asking who had washed it up as it was filthy dirty. It was just his way and I did love him because it is just his manner, he's a lovely guy, but I think he got tired at the end and the Lady C saga took its toll on him. He aged in there and I did worry for him; I think it was hard on him. Now with all the aggra-vation, mornings in the jungle are a strange time as everyone is apprehensive, you have to get yourself up and out of bed, you're tired, you get yourself ready, someone is going home, and then you find out who is doing the trial. As soon as the morning is done, you're fine and the days are great.

Susannah was adorable and I actually loved her hon-esty when she said that, now she'd got to know Vicky and me, she would be proud for us to meet her children. It made me happy that we had changed her perception of us. She gave her attention to everyone and I really liked her – she was very laid-back. I did manage a few Ferne-isms out there – like calling Yvette 'Yvonne' in a conversation (how I managed that when her name was on the back of her shirt I don't know!) – but by and large we all felt on a par with each other and Susannah and I shared our laid-back approach. Jorgie was sweet and gen-erous but on a different journey from me, as I think she struggled with being in there and I was loving it.

I was the queen of the pantry and I cleaned it every day – it was something to do and it kept the ants away. It was where we kept all our supplies and I liked the thought of it being shipshape and fresh. I also tried to make the most of the sun, though it moved around in a weird way so it was hard to catch it, and also there were a few people in there with vitiligo which meant that camp had to be in the shade a lot. George, Jorgie, Vic, Duncan and I were like sun worshippers, though it could be a battle to get the canopy down so we could top up our tans.

Brian was an amazing cook and when he went to Snake Rock the camp lost their chef, so I stepped in and people started to see that I could cook too, which was great. Later on as people began to get voted out we called it 'the curse of the cook' because whoever got voted to be chef, was evicted.

Chris Eubank openly wanted to win – he said it out loud to anyone who would listen that he wasn't there to make friends. He is very intelligent in the ring, he can work a man out instantly, but he can't navigate a puzzle or a task. He is good at giving advice but not the easiest to talk to.

I really liked Tony Hadley and I admired the way he took a lot of the flak for the Lady C thing; I genuinely believe he doesn't have a bad bone in his body. Like me, he absolutely loved the jungle and he reminded me of someone I would know back home. He is a great guy and my mum was delighted as she's always been such a huge fan.

Kieron Dyer was a sweet guy and had a lot of thoughts and a lot to say but we weren't that close as he had his group with Lady C and Chris. He also hated the jobs and wasn't that great at mucking in – though at least he was honest about not loving the chores. And then there was Lady C! The first thing to happen when I walked in the camp was that I was so nervous I knocked over a pot. She said: 'Oh no, we mustn't do that – we like it clean in here,' and I thought: Here we go! She's going to be a nightmare. In fact I ended up finding her fascinating and she just got me too. I like her, and I did pretty much from the start. I genuinely don't think she played up to it, she was what she was – she thought Tony was pointless and Duncan was a buffoon and that was that, really.

She loved the younger crowd and she was friends with Chris and Kieron. It was very black and white with her you were in or you were out. She was always kind to me and loved my cooking, and approval from Lady C was great – she made you want to be better, but she did like the rows as I think it helped her pass the time. In my opinion, and it is just my opinion, there wasn't bullying per se – it was just a lot of strong personalities and no filter. She had a persona of royalty and commanded respect, but she did seem older than she was – she was actually the same age as Duncan though it felt she was older, maybe because she was so slight. I was sad to see her go, but the situation did become draining and something had to give as it wasn't sustainable. Her parting shot was 'I will see you at the Versace'!

Obviously everyone could see how Vicky and I got on. I couldn't have wished for a better girl pal in there. She was so reassuring and generous. She was good fun too and I loved having someone to banter with. We didn't once talk about Charlie – why would we? He and I were over and done and what had or hadn't happened between them was irrelevant. It was a bit like the film *The Other Woman*, I love that girl and my jungle experience was 100 per cent made all the better for her having been in there with me. We ended up becoming the best of friends and we meet all the time and speak practically every day. It is so funny how things turn out and I'm so glad that, like me, she doesn't judge a book by its cover and we both gave each other a chance. I look forward to a lifelong friendship with her.

My connection with George was instant. We loved hanging out with each other. He explained the initial negative reaction we had received in camp in a bit more detail: he said the others had felt as if we'd swanned in and got everything on a plate while they had really struggled that helped to know it wasn't personal. I did really fancy him, but I realise now that everything is heightened in there so I wouldn't necessarily fancy him in the outside world; the main thing was that I just loved spending time with him, being young and silly. He was a breath of fresh air and he let me do his hair and muck about with his nails. However, he really struggled in there. He missed home and he had trouble with the lack of food; it got to a point where I would halve my portions and give it to either him or Keiron. The producers caught on to what was happening and set George and me on an overnight task – I did think he started to play up to the camera a bit, joking about it being our first date etc. Coming from a show like *TOWIE* I can spot it a mile off when someone stops being themselves, even just for a minute.

The thing about George was that when we left the jungle I developed severe separation anxiety and I missed him so much more than I'd thought was possible. I found it so hard to be away from him and I was confused about how we both felt. Something was not quite right. Later at the wrap party I asked him if he was gay, and he said no. I didn't ever say he was my boyfriend or that there was anything romantic going on, none the less my feelings for him were real and so accusations of a 'showmance' did hurt. It was a tight, platonic bond that will not be broken because I love being in his company.

I can genuinely say that I had time for everyone in the

camp, it was a fascinating group of people and all round one camp fire. It was amazing.

The people I was with in the camp obviously made up a huge chunk of my jungle experience, but the other main part involved the dreaded trials. There is no doubt – they were the worst part and far outweighed the hunger or living without any creature comforts. It is a weird one really, because it isn't just the actual trial itself that you end up dreading out there, it is the whole build up to finding out who the viewers have picked. There was constant worry on my part when I was picked more than once; were the viewers picking me because they really liked me or because they found me annoying? Had I set my fate in that first trial when I had screamed and shown how much I hated the box task? Either way, I was determined never to walk away from any trial I was nominated for, and I didn't.

In one of my initial interviews, the producers had asked if I had any specific fears and I was happy to say no. I was honestly one of those viewers who would watch the trials from the comfort of my own sofa, drinking a cup of tea, thinking 'I could do that', and that it couldn't be as bad as they made out. I was sure that, for the sake of TV, a lot of talking-up went on. Well, how wrong was I?!

As I have said, my first experience of a trial was the one I did with Vicky and Spencer. The second trial, 'Horri-flying Circus', was with Vicky on the high wire: I had to balance up on a wire, blindfolded, listening to the instructions Vicky gave me as I unscrewed the stars and passed them to her to put in a bag. It was the definition of being thrown in at the deep-end as I had to immediately put such trust in someone I hardly knew. In a way it was lucky I was blindfolded; I genuinely had no idea how high up we were. We knew that the person who received the highest number of votes from the public was the one who had to wear the blindfold, so from the off it was clear that the viewers were picking me for the entertainment value. Despite the fact that I'd won the first trial, I had done all that screaming and, though it was totally genuine, I guess I had played into the hands of the viewers who wanted drama. The trials did cause me genuine anxiety – I put so much pressure on myself not to let anyone down and I was truly terrified of the unknown. Lady C also got picked a lot but that didn't always offer me comfort – often as soon as Ant and Dec would tell her she had been picked, they would follow it up by informing the camp that she was exempt on health grounds. As soon as this happened, I knew I was next in line.

Anyway, back to my balancing act. It was a really tricky task as, despite the fact there weren't really any hideous creatures to deal with, it needed such concentration and co-ordination and I couldn't see a thing. The last stars involved getting into a box with green ants that bit really badly, so I was brushing them off, balancing, and still try-ing to unscrew the star. I was so panicked by the ants that I dropped the final star, and I was gutted that we went back to camp with just over half. We were still the 'new girls' and we wanted to prove that we had what it took to go the distance, and that we were team players who could hold our own. But we gave it our best shot – that's all you can do in there – and they were a great bunch who didn't judge you on how many meals you came back with. As long as you tried your best, that was good enough.

Trial number three for me was the first one on my own – this, as well as the one I did with Vicky, was voted for by the public. I didn't ever really get used to that sick fear that hit the pit of my stomach when my name was called out, but I did develop a little routine to help psyche myself up. You were also allowed to pick which two other celebs from the camp would walk you to the draw-bridge before you set off. It mattered to me who that was as, often, they would give you a little pep talk before you left camp. I would usually ask for George and Vicky as they were very positive and upbeat. I certainly needed it for the third trial, ominously named 'Floods of Fear'.

It was always a giveaway that the trial was underground if you arrived at the clearing and you couldn't see anything in front of you! I got there and talked it through with Ant and Dec and Dr Bob, but all I could see were pipes, tunnels and sewers – it did not bode well. My eyes then caught sight of these reptiles that were lying flat and skimming the bottom – it took me a while to realise that they were giant and disgusting eels, and size-wise they were beyond anything you could imagine. Suddenly, more dropped out of some of the tunnels and I had a massive panic. I could feel myself welling up – never had a task been so well-named and sheer terror washed over me. The fear was real and took over – I started to have a panic attack at what I was facing. I suppose it was the first one I'd done on my own and the enormity had suddenly hit me. Dr Bob came and talked me through the trial but I turned my back and started to cry. I was determined not to give anyone any ammunition to label me the 'weak one' and I remember saying: 'Please don't film me'. I was putting on a front but everyone could see I was suffering – they were great and gave me the option to pull out, but that wasn't going to happen and that was when I first said, 'Feel the fear and do it anyway' – something that was to become my catchphrase. I got on my helmet, knee and elbow pads, and stood on the silver ladder waiting for them to say 'Go'.

I had under ten minutes to do it and I lowered myself into these different chambers that were all coming from one tunnel. There was hardly any space and I had to crouch like a crab and creep along because the tunnel was so low. I had to squeeze my body through these small openings that were surrounded by black Velcro. There were different creatures in each chamber: spider crabs in one, toads in another (leading to the comedy moment where I mistook the toads for frogs and actually started apologising to them for nearly stepping on them).

As I was down there, I gave myself a good pep talk before plunging my hand through the penultimate chamber full of snakes, and unscrewing the stars. I finished that one knowing they must have saved the best for last, and was told I had a minute and a half to tackle the final chamber. I had done everything thrown at me down there and I couldn't imagine what horror the last chamber contained. Imagine my delight when I realised it was holding an actual crocodile! It was just a baby, so I was told, but it looked huge. I put my head through the hole, saw it flinch, and I just thought, 'Nah'. I could still hear Ant and Dec's words of encouragement (as well as telling me not to tread on it even though there wasn't a spare inch of ground). By the time I had worked out what was going on, I only had twenty seconds left and I reasoned with myself that I had done well enough winning ten out of a possible twelve stars. Also, getting ten stars for a camp of twelve doesn't mean that two people don't eat – it just means smaller portions.

Next came the 'Panic Pit' and originally, Lady C got picked to do this trial when she first arrived in camp, but she was later excused on medical grounds. What people don't always realise is that these trials cost a lot of money and a lot of thought goes into designing them – they are key to the show and are thought out in minute detail. So imagine how they feel if someone turns up for a trial, takes one look at it, and just says, 'No thanks!'. Calling the 'I'm a Celebrity' card or just not even trying means that the audience have a whole show with no trial entertainment, and also means that everyone in the crew have prepared to film a trial that doesn't happen. The head honcho of trials, Matt, is a legend and he actually told me at the wrap party that I was one of his favourite trialists – he said it was obvious that I genuinely loathed doing them but I always gave it everything and provided the real entertainment factor by just getting on with the job in hand. I was so proud when he said that – it was the perfect way to be remembered from my time on the show.

With a name like 'Panic Pit', I knew immediately that it was another underground one. I had to crawl along on my backside down a slope to get into a coffin-shaped pit they had dug into the ground. You could just about sit up in it but, realistically, you had to be horizontal so you could strap yourself in. There was a *window painted screen* to my left and two entrances and exits (there was a quick exit in case of an emergency but they preferred you to crawl across the whole pit for maximum drama). To my left were the cameras behind some glass and I had two funnels by my head to let the creatures in. A this point I didn't know what they were or how many would be joining me. In my head I prepared for everything under the sun to be put in with me. The task was to lie there for eight minutes, with all the creatures they added in and, all of a sudden, these different-sized pythons started coming in. They were a mixture of sizes and weights but all I could think about were the small, erratic ones – there were over 40 of them, all lying around and on top of me.

Initially they had dropped in all this sand, that was a shock in itself, but the snakes just kept coming. I became so rigid that everything seized up and, as each minute passed, the sense of achievement was so real and I knew this was my chance to show how much grit I had. In a way, I see now that the girl in that hole was the absolute opposite of the heartbroken girl Charlie finished with. That shattered girl who couldn't eat or sleep and could barely function. That girl was showing the nation real guts and I felt the strongest I'd ever been.

I knew that things were intense because there wasn't a lot of chat, especially as one of the smaller snakes slithered onto my face and wrapped itself round my neck in a way that meant half of it was under my nose, getting in the way of my breathing. I remember shouting out: 'Guys!! It's on my face!'. It was so heavy and I could feel them creeping all over me, their skin was so thick and they each weighed a tonne. They reassured me that it was okay and that I wasn't in danger, but I didn't realise that in their earpieces they were being told it was possible they would have to pull the trial at any moment.

Psychologically, they were also worried about how I was coping being in there but were soon reassured by the fact that I made a joke about having a Britney Spears moment!

My whole body froze; it was tight and my neck was at a weird angle, as I wanted to make sure that I exposed as little skin as possible. For the last two minutes they turned off the lights in the pit, but my eyes had been shut for the whole six minutes I had already been in there, so it didn't make much difference. I was doing my usual childbirth-like noises to get me through and, as soon as they lifted the top off, I screamed: 'Get me out!'

As I climbed out I was overwhelmed by a huge sense of relief and such pride that I had won every star, and that was compounded by the look on the faces of Ant and Dec – their shocked expressions said it all and it is still the trial that most viewers ask me about when they stop me on the street. So many of them say they watched it from behind a cushion as it was so tense.

I went back to camp with eight stars and I was on a high – I couldn't wait to tell them all – but as soon as I stepped back over the bridge, the mood felt immediately heavy and ominous. My joy was short-lived as I found out that Lady C had left. I felt genuinely sad she had gone but when the food came down that night, more than ever it was the best feeling to see how much was there – every minute I had suffered had been worth it.

Making the final was the most extraordinary feeling in the world. In my mind there had been every chance I would be out first. It was never my aim to get there – genuinely all I wanted to do was the slide and I would have been happy! The final ended up being the dream three and I felt a bigger sense of achievement than I ever thought possible. I still pinch myself now, and I truly believe the Australian jungle was a lifeline for me. It exposes you for what and who you really are; it is impossible to be anything but yourself in there. The public knows it is getting the real deal from everyone who goes in there; which is just one of the reasons it continues to go from strength to strength. It was truly one of the best times of my life and I will be forever grateful.

Epilogue
Good Vibes Only

Coming back from Australia at the airport I was mobbed – there were all different age groups – and I became known as Ferne from the jungle. It still feels like a bit of a dream and it was totally overwhelming. Going through my messages, all I can remember was feeling: My God, people really like me.

Instantly I knew it was time to leave *TOWIE*. Another series felt like I would have been taking a step back. I had been a part of the jungle – an amazing show that I really felt allowed me to be myself, in which I hadn't become the bad guy. Going back to *TOWIE* would be a risk, and one bad scene would have set me right back to the start.

I bumped into one of the execs at Nanny Pat's funeral and thought it wasn't the time or the place to have the discussion, though she made it clear that they expected it to be business as usual. I had gone to the jungle under the proviso that I would always go back to the show, but coming out I realised that it didn't excite me any more. We had the meeting and it was great; they were so honest and said they just wanted a piece of the jungle Ferne. I would never turn my back on the show that made me, and *TOWIE* did that for me, but there is always a time to move on and this was it for me. But they had been good to me and we agreed an exit strategy that worked for everyone.

I love to work. You saw it in the jungle, that I'm a worker; I've always had a job and I really believe there is nothing more satisfying than doing a hard day's graft and getting paid. There is a lot of pressure on the cast to get a business or extend their shelf life, as people say that the fame won't last for ever, but why shouldn't it last for ever? I have always thought that it'll last as long as you want it to because you get out what you put in.

In a way not much has changed post-*TOWIE* and yet everything has turned on its head. I have learned that there is only one Ferne McCann and I am still it, good and bad, maybe just a slightly different version. I still make mistakes, I still put my foot in it and say things as I see them rather than how they should be said. I have learned a lot and the hard way, but I've also started to realise I don't have to be so hard on myself – I am a kind and decent girl who went into a show like *TOWIE* and got sucked into behaving in a certain way that didn't always show my best side. But I never forget that no one made me join and no one ever put words in my mouth. Part of what's happened to me since I came into the public eye is that I now understand being an adult involves owning my behaviour and decisions.

What do I think of *TOWIE* now? That's simple: it's the best thing that ever happened to me and I will be forever grateful for how it changed my life for the better. Without it I know I wouldn't have any of the incredible opportunities on offer to me or some of my best friendships. I wanted what the show had to offer and went after it. Yes, it ended up being more than I could handle at times, but mostly it was the most incredible journey.

I have tried to be as honest as I can about the show and the pluses and minuses of being on such a successful series. I never want to blame the show for the things that have happened to me – the good far outweighs the bad in my opinion. I knew there were risks when I joined but, ultimately, I made decisions about how to behave and interpret the situations I was confronted with and sometimes they weren't the right ones. But that's life.

I think since I broke my ankle and started to see my spiritual advisor, Carol, I have calmed down a bit. Without getting too deep, I've begun to believe the universe has its own rules and ways and plans and that things do truly happen for a reason. We have to accept and deal with the bad to get to the good and, though things have sometimes felt dark (especially in the bad patches on the show), I couldn't be happier with where I am now. Some of those worst times on *TOWIE* that almost broke me also kept me on air and in the public consciousness, eventually allowing me the chance to go into the jungle. That has led me on to my work on *This Morning* and all the other things that are out there for me. In those months after the jungle, when people asked what my job was, the thrill of being able to say that I was a TV presenter was immense.

When it comes to relationships, again, I've always worn my heart on my sleeve and in this book I have tried to be honest. I will always love and adore Charlie;

he was my best friend and I hope he always will be. He taught me how to love and also how to get through heart-break without being bitter. I am in a much better frame of mind now to be able to see the beauty of the relation-ship we had. Before it went wrong, what we'd had was pure and uncomplicated. This is a man who, knowing I didn't have a phone to communicate if I needed a lift back from Brentwood station after a work night out in London, went there anyway and sat in the car park until the very last train came in from Liverpool Street with me on it. His only aim was to make sure I got home safely and if that meant sitting in an empty car park for hours, then so be it. People often ask if we will get back together as, at the time of writing this, we are both single. My answer is I don't think so. What we had was to be cele-brated, but we are different from before and going backwards isn't something I think would be right for either of us.

One of the best things about doing this book has been the chance to reflect honestly on my life so far. It has opened my eyes and taught me things about myself; I can see certain patterns of behaviour with boys that I will think about changing going forward. It has taught me to trust in myself, to surround myself with good friends and live every day to the full. My time in the jungle was a blessing and something I am grateful for every day – I haven't really kept in touch with many of the contestants in there, but I see Vicky all the time. I think we have a special bond because we were the outsiders – I feel very lucky to have made that strong female friendship with her.

As for me, I am a young woman still finding her way and learning; I still make mistakes; I still don't think I'll ever understand boys! But I'm working on myself. In the end you can't always control what happens to you but you can control how you react to it, and that involves deciding what you give your energy to and what you involve yourself in.

I actually feel happy, strong and purposeful. I love my time on *This Morning* and have been amazed and humbled by all the things that have come my way. I also have become an aunty for the first time when my beautiful sister Sophie gave birth to gorgeous Ronnie. It's the most amazing thing to have this new life in the family and we are all so close because of him. I look forward to being an important part of his life. He will definitely have fun times with Aunty Ferne!

I might have left *TOWIE* but I still love and celebrate

everything about Essex and will be living here, in my own place, for a long time yet. Being part of the show meant that an extraordinary thing happened to a lot of us when we joined, and to have shared that with my close friends was amazing. We were a group of young, naïve and ambitious kids trying to live the dream – I feel truly grateful that I am still living it.

Acknowledgements

Leisa Maloney – my magic. Together we are Magic McCann and Magic Maloney. My fierce, loyal manager. Where would I be without you? Thank you for keeping my life in check and always having my best interests at heart. Thank you for being patient and listening and always sticking by me. You are more to me than a manager, you are my friend and make me 'howl' like no other. You always put things into perspective and give me the best advice. You are so incredibly trustworthy and positive. Thank you for having a vision, never giving up, and thank you to the universe for bringing her into my life . . . Seriously would be lost without you, Leis.

Carly Cook – I can't quite believe we have a book! You are one of the most selfless and dedicated individuals that I have ever met. Thank you for capturing my voice perfectly – you understand and just get me, it's that simple. I have loved our long sessions whilst writing this book but have felt sorry for you on occasion as I can go off on a tangent and be a bit crazy at times. I hope you have enjoyed this process as much as I have, you hard-working little thing.

Mummy – you are my number one person in this whole entire universe. What a journey we have had. At times I know I can be exhausting and you worry but, my God, do we have fun?! Thank you for encouraging me to always be myself, for nurturing my weird and wonderful ways, for putting up with me. I owe you everything. You're kind, non-judgemental, patient and strong. I have everything to thank you for.

Sophie – my big sister. You have been there through everything, thick and thin! Thank you for putting up with me! Thank you for often keeping me calm and putting things into perspective. You have always been the wise one, and thank you for always allowing me to turn to you whenever I have needed you. Thank you for making me an aunty. I love my nephew to the moon and back, he is my angel. Thank you to Ian too as if it wasn't for him, Ronnie wouldn't be here! Haha. Plus Ian, thank you for being patient with me! You and Soph always make time for me and I am so grateful. I love you both.

To everyone at Century – particularly Ajda Vucicevic, Selina Walker, Jason Smith, Gemma Bareham, Jessica Gulliver, Sarah Ridley and the rest of the team. I will always be so grateful to have been given the chance to tell my story, in my own words. Having my autobiography published is a dream come true.

Charlie Sims – thank you for teaching me how to love. No one can ever take what we had away from us! We were each other's first loves and are Puppy Pandas for life! You will always hold a very special place in my heart.

Grandad – what a man. You are the most level-headed, kind and patient man in my life. If ever I need you, you are always there, willing to listen and to give advice. Thank you for supporting Mum, Soph and me through-out the years – we really would be lost without you. I love that even though you are in your eighties you are so active and keep yourself so young. You are an inspiration. You are a complete social butterfly and always at every party – all of my friends love you! You are not just *my* grandad, you are a grandad to everyone.

Dad – firstly, thank you for bringing me into this world with Mama. Thank you for teaching me how to laugh and live. We are so similar in many ways and I love how much we laugh when we get together. You are always the life and soul of the party and I have always aspired to be the same. I am truly grateful for the start you gave me and Sophie and how you continue to support both of us, even if you don't always agree.

Nanny, Nanna and Grandad Bert – my dearest grandparents who have passed. I have so many fond memories of you all. Thank you for being incredible, fun grandparents – we were truly lucky to spend such quality time with you growing up. If only you were here to see what I was up to now. All those shows in the living room and endless singing that you put up with have all been worthwhile.

Sue Wells – thank you for totally being there for me in my teen years, your door was always open for me and I will be forever grateful to you.

My nearest and dearest –

Stace – my Number One main chick, thank you for being so loyal. I have had, I think, possibly too much fun with you! I love you so much, bubs. Sorry for never letting you go home on a Sunday (it's because I always want you with me).

Sophie – my everything. The love I have for you is too much to write here! Thank you for being a weird partner in crime with me, thank you for singing with me, thank you for your creativity and thank you for always being there!

Gem – thank you for being so loyal, caring and kind! Your funny little ways make me giggle like no other. I love you.

Jerri – thank you for being a fierce friend. It's as simple as that! Thank you for never judging and thank you for always putting a smile on my face, love u toots.

Abi – thank you for your kind heart and thank you for always putting others first.

Steph – thank you for always being positive and finding fun in every situation. Love you.

Sarah Newn – thank you for always making me laugh with the randomness you send me over WhatsApp. Love you sassy girl, my trap queen.

Carl – little did you know when we met in Ibiza what you were getting yourself into. Although we have only been friends for three years, I couldn't imagine life without my Carl. I am sure I have driven you to distraction on more than one occasion but, my God, do we have fun! I can honestly say you feel like part of my family, always honest and fiercely loyal, I love you baby boy xx.

Martin Frizel & Jess – thank you for giving me the opportunity at *This Morning*, my first presenting job of many I hope. Thank you for giving me my first gig, I have learned and grown so much at *This Morning* and I am truly grateful for that.

Danielle – thank you for making me laugh until my belly hurts. I love your spirit. Thank you for sharing that with me and thank you for our hour-long phone calls. I never get bored.

Thanks to the universe. I thank you every day of my life so it would make sense to thank you here. Thank you. I am grateful. Always.

Claire, Kenny and Matilda – thank you for being such supportive, special family friends, I love you all!

Lesley, Pierre, Robyn and Dan – I have known you for what feels like my whole life. Thank you for being such wonderful friends to me and my family throughout the years. Thank you for the laughs and memories from our 'McMoly' holidays. You have always encouraged me to be myself and I am grateful for your love!

Auntie Sandra – thank you for always being so generous and kind. You have always treated Sor... and me as if we were your own. We have had some amazing days out and holidays over the years, thank you. I love our chats, you are such a loyal and peaceful person and I have learned a lot from you.

Lyndsey at MUA – thank you for putting up with me whilst I'm sitting in front of the mirror moaning about my wonky face. Your make-up and hair always makes me feel incredible.

Daniella, the wonderful exec on TOWIE – thank you for listening, supporting and just getting me. You are an incredible woman and I am lucky to have worked with you on the show.

Rach Hardy – Rach, since day one of me joining *TOWIE*, we clicked. You have tirelessly had my back, supported me and understood my vision. Thank you babes.

Chloe Mcgee and Justin Jeffreys – Thank you for making me laugh and having my back, the pair of you.

The *I'm a Celeb* crew: Micky, Paul and David – You cast me on one of my favourite shows: it was the best experience of my life to date and I have you all to thank for giving me the opportunity of a lifetime.

Carol, my spiritual healer – I am so grateful you came into my life. Thank you for introducing me to the wonderful world of spirituality. You have made me look at life from another angle, introduced me to the angels and taught me so much. Thank you.

Geri Padalino – thank you for being so supportive from the very beginning of *TOWIE*. Although it didn't work out at Sassoon's, you were the one who encouraged me to take the opportunity and to just go for it and I'm grateful for that.

Sam – thank you for always making me see sense, you have always put things into perspective for me when I felt like life wasn't going according to plan. Thank you for your calming influence because, my God, I have needed it over the years. Thank you for all the good times growing up, I have the most incredible memories that I will never forget. Love you. x

Billie – where do I start? Maybe with simply thanking you for being my friend. Thank you for endlessly supporting me and tirelessly having my back. You got me from the get go and I got you, my ink to my blink, my

Ant to my Dec, my yin to my yang, haha. Thank god we met when we did in year 7 as I couldn't imagine life without you. Unfortunately you're stuck with me as we are forever friends. God, I love you Bill!

Jess Wright – thank you for your spontaneous get-up-and-go spirit. Jess, in the recent years you have been there for me and been a loyal, true friend – thank you. Love you.

Gemma Collins – thank you for always championing me. You always have belief in me and encourage me to do the impossible. Thank you.

Lydia Bright – thank you for always being so positive, supportive and congratulating. I have never met someone who is capable of always being so happy for others and selfless. You are a bloody good girl and good things will happen to you. I'm glad you are my friend boo x

Quick shout out to the Blue Storm netball girls and to the Gatsby crew. Thank you for welcoming me into the musical world with open arms. You have all been a dream.

Lastly, to my school teacher, Mr Ninian – thank you for teaching me not only the subject of English but that I can succeed at anything if I put my mind to it.

Photographic Acknowledgements

First plate section:

Pages 1–7 – © Author's own

Page 8 – 'This was my 24th birthday' – © Getty Images

Second plate section:

Page 1 – Feeling very *Sex in the City* for my blog –
© Author's own

'Glamming it up for Godzilla' – © Getty Images

Page 2 – 'Glamour line-up for the TV Choice Awards' –
© Getty Images

'First year at the NTAs' – ©Simon Burcell/Splash
Images

Page 3 – *I'm a Celebrity* – © ITV/Rex/Shutterstock

Page 4 – 'One of my favourite shots from my blog' –
© Author's own

'My first presenting job on *This Morning*' – ©ITV/
Rex/Shutterstock

Page 5 – 'Me looking glamourous at *The Amazing
Spiderman 2* premiere' – © WENN

Page 6 – 'This was for the *TOWIE* calendar and one of
my first shoots' – © Lime Pictures

'This is from this year's NTAs. This was such a great
night' – © Justin Goff/GoffPhotos.com

Page 7 – 'This is me channelling my Riviera look' –
© Getty Images

Page 8 – © Author's own